UNDER THE BUS

*Why Women Hurt Women
in Business... And, How to Change It*

Patricia Blakey

Copyright © 2015 Patricia Blakey
All Rights Reserved Worldwide
ISBN-13: 978-1517174521
ISBN-10: 1517174521

Cover art, design, book graphics and formatting by Dan Price, Austin, TX. To contact Dan, please go to his website danprice139.wix.com/artofdanprice.

For workshops or speaking engagements with Patricia, email info@underthebusnomore.com

No part of this manuscript may be copied or transmitted in any format, including physical or digital version without expressed written permission of the publisher.

Disclaimer

I am not a therapist. This book is based on my research and personal experience as a professional in business for over twenty-five years. It is based on over 300 formal and informal interviews of women in various sized businesses in varying industries and occupations.

I have worked in marketing, sales, business development, recruiting and consulting for startups, small to medium sized businesses and Fortune 500 companies. I also worked as an advocate at a domestic violence shelter. I am a business and life coach and a mentor.

The term "under the bus syndrome™ or "UBS™ is not a psychological term. It describes a trend in business that is predominately displayed by certain women as referenced in the book.

This book is not to meet the therapeutic needs of the reader. However, this may be a useful book in discussions with an human resources professional, women's groups and organizations, your place of business or with a business coach.

This book can help women no matter where they are in their career to become aware of Under the Bus Syndrome™ and learn strategies to personally empower themselves and other women in the process.

No part of this book may be copied electronically or in any other form without the written permission of the publisher.

Table of Contents

Acknowledgements	4
Section I	
Thrown Under The Bus No More	8
Chapter One: Tire Tracks on My Back	12
Chapter Two: Herstory of Under the Bus™ and Under the Bus Syndrome™ (UBS)™	14
Chapter Three: What is UBS™?	20
Section II	
Reasons, Stories and Solutions: Tire Tracks on Women's Backs	26
What's Driving It: Scarcity Mentality	27
o Tire Tracks: Talia	34
o Tire Tracks: Liz	38
o Tire Tracks: Jennifer	41
• Suggested Solutions	43
What's Driving It: Women's Image Issues	60
o Tire Tracks: Christie	65
o Tire Tracks: Amy	68
o Tire Tracks: Esther	71
• Suggested Solutions	74
What's Driving It: Masculine Versus Feminine Acceptance	77
o Tire Tracks: Rachel	83
o Tire Tracks: Mary Jane	85
o Tire Tracks: Janet	88
• Suggested Solutions	92
Chapter Four: Telltale Signs -You're Going Under the Bus	97
Chapter Five: A Strong Woman Versus An UBSer™	99
Chapter Six: The Effects of UBS and Tire Tracks on Business	101
Chapter Seven: Get on the Bus and Drive toward a Better Future	106
Chapter Eight: To a Better Future	108

Acknowledgements

Special thanks to Chris Liaguno, Somatic Therapist and Authentic Response Coach and friend for providing insights, causes and suggesting solutions to this syndrome and supporting a different way of being for women in business. Thanks to Dr. Debra Wingfield (my mentor), Mari Van Natta, Linda Hannafious, Colleen Gerity, Cindy Lau, Kenyetta Bond, James Sorrells, Matt Albright, Sharon and Doug Goldhirsch for their support, love and encouragement in the process of writing this book. Heartfelt thanks to all the women who shared their stories and their willingness to let the experience transform their lives for the positive.

Love, blessings and gratitude to my family, friends, furry friends (dogs and cat – yes, I needed to clarify), fellow writers of "elephant-in-the-room topics," my ninth grade English teacher, Mrs. Janet Richards, the journalism/communications professors at Colorado State University, former business associates and colleagues and the countless number of women and men, I interviewed for this book or had long discussions about it. And, to all those whom I met and encouraged me to write on.

I would like to extend a special blessing to those women of whom this book is written. May your eyes, ears and hearts be open to receive and believe another way of being through internal validation where you may bring peace, productivity and progress to all the women and men around you while you feel empowered too. Or, at least ladies, stop throwing other women under the bus! Amen.

For Lillian and Stella

SECTION I

Section I
THROWN UNDER THE BUS NO MORE

When I began writing this book, it was more of a cathartic release for me and I had no intention about my experience becoming a book. It was an effort to release my anger, sadness and shock. I also wanted to come to an understanding and acceptance of it so I could move on with my life and use the methods and teachings that I had learned to continue to be at peace with myself and those around me.

After I began sharing my experiences with other women, I found too that they had or were experiencing the same situations with other women in business as I had. I told them I thought about researching and writing a book about it. They too found the behavior as perplexing as I did, wanted answers and ways to avoid it, deal with it or resource themselves and their daughters so it didn't perpetuate.

As a business woman, author, coach, executive search consultant, advocate at a domestic violence shelter and marketing consultant with over 25 years of experience in the business world, I was determined to identify the problem, get to its root causes and find ways to empower women so the effects would not be so devastating for them, their jobs or the companies and organizations which they represent.

Having conducted formal and informal interviews of over 300 women, I discovered a trend and called it a syndrome. I studied the reasons and conferred with a psychotherapist. The result was to develop solutions that would empower women beginning at any age and at any time of life.

In countless discussions with businessmen and therapists, they also pointed to the fact that the empowerment of women needed to be done without disparaging men. In truth, after reading this you will see that in many instances, one of the biggest reasons for women not succeeding in business is how we unconsciously treat each other and this stems from how we treat ourselves.

It is true there is still not complete equality in pay structures, organizational dynamics and other aspects of business. This book focuses on identifying the instances when women are treating other women unjustly through actual case studies. It looks at the reasons why women do not treat other women fairly. Lastly, it makes real life suggestions on how women can feel and act empowered. Although the suggestions are listed in particular sections, any or all of them can be used at any time.

The information in this book comes from my personal experiences and lessons from working with coaches, mentors, business men and women, spiritual teachers and practitioners. My journey is about living from the inside out or the ability to internally validate. I learned how to become centered within myself no matter what is going on around me. And, you can too.

The stories and the information illustrate actual samples of women from varying industries and professions experiencing Under the Business Syndrome™.

Again, I was hesitant in turning this into a book. I am not stating that all women behave poorly towards other women in business. It is, however, pervasive enough that it needs to be explored. One of my best friend's, Linda told me, "don't worry if there is backlash, conflict or heated discussion about this book. Realize that it opens the door for change and healing."

I could have written a book about our individual and collective anger, a need to be right or victimhood, how women were first repressed by men, then by each other and let's complain about it. My message is much more positive in its outlook. Rather this is a book about discovering ways for women to internally validate, connect to their higher selves and/or a higher power to feel empowered. Emmett Fox summarizes it beautifully in his booklet, The Golden Key, "study and research are well in their own time and place, but no amount of either will get you out of a concrete difficulty. Nothing but practical work in your own consciousness will do that."

The stories in this book are true based on my interviews (names are changed) and are meant primarily to shed light on Under the Bus Syndrome™. The majority of the stories are omitted from this book for a reason. The reason for the omission is threefold; 1.There are enough stories to identify UBS™; 2.This book illustrates the causes and focuses on the solutions; and 3.The solution portion focuses on ways we can live and act on purpose and be empowered, so we can help future generations of businesswomen to feel empowered so they in turn, empower other women.

Let the journey begin.

Chapter One
TIRE TRACKS ON MY BACK

I was sitting on the patio looking out into the wooded area surrounding my townhome wondering how I had just lost my job. It hadn't been so long since I had moved 3,000 miles from my family and friends to take this job.

How could I begin to sort out my feelings? I was stunned. My ego was bruised. I was worried about being able to pay my bills. How could I face calling my family and friends to tell them the bad news? I loved my job and had given it my all.

I had been commended by upper management, vendors and clients on how I had completely turned the department around for the better. I had the respect of my team.

The company was thriving and growing, there was huge interest in our new product line and the stock was at one of its highest levels in company history. However, these successes did not stop my boss from firing me that cold winter's day.

Several weeks prior to the firing, my boss kept telling me that I was doing a fantastic job. "I'm afraid for my job," she would say to me repeatedly in conversation. A few weeks earlier, she asked me to stop copying the CEO on any of my documents. She then asked me to write the annual plans for the department and products which were her responsibility. I thought the request was odd because she had just returned from a leave of absence. I did not want to challenge her on the request, however, so I diligently began to work on it.

I spent many hours researching, strategizing and collaborating with all my vendor contacts to create two plans inclusive of all actions that needed to be taken and by whom, timeframes, resources, staffing, budgets, estimated return on investment and contingency plans. I had made suggestions on covering different industry sectors having made contact with the top influencers in those sectors to understand how best to market to them. I had great relationships with all my vendors so they provided the best options possible to mutually grow our businesses. I felt a huge sense of accomplishment in completing those two major documents for the company.

I sent both of these documents to my boss and did not copy the CEO as instructed. I worked night and day to complete the work and I was very happy to present them to her although I still wondered why she had not written them herself. I did not want to be insubordinate so I never questioned her about it.

The next week I was fired and she was promoted to Senior Vice President. She had deliberately set me up. I had experienced Under the Bus Syndrome™ first hand, but I didn't know it at the time.

Chapter Two
"HERSTORY" OF UNDER THE BUS™ AND UNDER THE BUS SYNDROME™

Most of us are optimistic when we enter the workforce. There is great satisfaction in knowing that you can take care of yourself and your family. It is also gratifying to know that you are challenged by your chosen profession and that you are contributing to the company. Ultimately, most of us enjoy serving others and thriving in the process. This optimism leads many of us, including me, to believe a boss will be someone who wants his or her employees to succeed, gives them the necessary tools to do so, and will support and lead.

Initially, I resented hearing about "the good ole' boys club (GOBC)". Gloria Steinem, feminist, activist and a visionary in the women's equality movement and I had more in common than I thought. However, over the years, and there have been over 25 years in business, I came to admire a few of the dynamics and principles of the GOBC. Men were helping men succeed in business. In fact, many men became mentors for other men and showed them the ropes by introducing each other to their business associates and networks. They would bring the other men in on deals, teaching them new ways of doing business and forming friendships that often lasted a lifetime.

Why haven't women formed a "Good ole Girls Network'?
Historically, there have been fewer jobs for women. Women entered the workforce during World War II due to necessity. During the following decades women entered the workforce because they wanted to earn a living, out of economic necessity, to be independent, to be challenged and contribute to society in new and creative

ways. Men have long been established as business professionals. They have been conditioned as young boys to go for what they want and pursue it until they achieve it. If they cannot get what they want out of their current professional situation, they will go elsewhere. Economic uncertainty has changed this dynamic slightly where men will stay at jobs due to monetary concerns but will make plans to leave as soon as they have something else lined up.

Men have utilized their masculinity to be aggressive, strong, courageous, competitive, and persistent. They don't stay in situations or deals that don't serve them and they don't care if they're rejected or show it as readily. They are driven by providing for themselves and their families. They are not typically afraid of conflict in business (resolving conflict with their wives, girlfriends or partners – that is a different subject), but typically don't harbor it once, it's discussed. Men will mentor other men and help them get ahead in business. Although, these are sweeping generalities and may not hold as true in the current state of the economy, especially concerning "going elsewhere", it does speak to the foothold men have in business.

"Many women were forced or felt like they were forced to be more like men – bitchy, competitive, and aggressive. The Good Old Boys Club (GOBC) was closed to women and only became open to women who would exhibit primarily what is thought of as masculine characteristics," said Chris Liaguno, psychotherapist. Women have not been in the workforce that long. This stems back to the time in history that was alluded to earlier in this book. During World War II, there was a huge influx of women entering the workforce to manufacture weapons and to keep industry going in the United States while the vast majority of men were overseas at war.

When the men returned home from war, many of the women continued to work. Women liked their independence and providing extra income. However, the traditional family model of the 1940s and 1950s had the majority of men being the bread winners and the majority of women being homemakers. Young women began to enter the workforce for a greater sense of independence and liberation from the old model of looking at the world. There was a fresh idealism towards freedom of what women could do in society.

The number and types of jobs for women during the 20th century was limited. Fewer jobs meant more competition and some women became overly ambitious and competitive, jealous and conniving when it came to mentoring or fostering networks with other women. Women overcompensated for the fact that they weren't getting higher level jobs and on the off chance they did, these women were paid significantly less than their male counterparts. They often viewed other women as a threat or a rival – not as a peer. The scarcity mentality was alive and well.

Since the 1980s, the advancement of women in the corporate ranks was slow with less than 10% of women holding executive level positions. The reasons for this could include a sexist glass ceiling but that is most likely not the primary reason as originally thought.

Primarily women were not taking educational courses or being groomed for those executive positions. Also, women were not taught how to envision career and other goals at that time because there were limited female executive role models.

Fast forward thirty years and the number of women not advancing to executive ranks as quickly as their levels of education and talent would assume is perplexing indeed.

According to a Catalyst survey dated published in December of 2013, "Women currently hold 4.6 percent of Fortune 500 CEO positions and 4.6 percent of Fortune 1000 CEO positions."

An excerpt from the article by Alanna Vagianos from The Huffington Post entitled "There are Still Few Women at the Top of Fortune 500 Companies," further addresses the Catalyst survey.

"Ilene H. Lang, President and CEO of Catalyst, explained in a press release that the lack of women at the top of Fortune 500 companies is not due to a supply problem: "There are plenty of qualified women ready for board and top executive positions, as some companies have proven. It's important [to hire women into these positions] and it's not hard."

At the end of 2013, many leadership teams and corporate boards are still all-male staffed. Out of the top Fortune 500 companies, 135 still have no female executive officers. These all-male companies include big-name brands such as Apple, Delta Air Lines, Exxon Mobile and Google. As Lang noted in the same press release, successful business performance is linked to diverse leadership, making these numbers more than a bit perplexing."

The lack of advancement of women in the corporate ranks makes me wonder if the phenomenon of women throwing other women under the bus in the workplace is much more pervasive than my interviews and research could have imagined.

For purposes of this book, it is noted that not all females in business experience UBS™. However, through personal experiences as well as speaking with countless women on the subject, there are a staggering number of women who have experienced female bosses, co-workers and staff members who exhibit signs of UBS™. Regardless of the type of industry or professions, this syndrome is affecting day-to-day business. Whether it is loss of productivity, low morale, office gossip, bullying, prohibition of creativity, employees quitting or any host of other negative effects, UBS™, if not brought to light can completely debilitate teams, departments and entire companies.

According to Alanna Vagianos' article as noted prior there is another problem that may be a result of women not in the executive ranks. "Previous research has shown that without female business leaders, there's a lack of role models to encourage young women looking to enter the business world."

In a 2014 survey of a group of women business professionals on the social media site Linkedin.com, the majority of respondents did not specify a gender preference when it came to a boss or supervisor. The primary characteristics that were exhibited by a great boss were mutual respect and trust. Respondents mentioned that they had experienced excellent and horrible bosses from both genders. However, there were a high percentage of respondents who mentioned that they had experienced more than one female boss who was horrible and preferred to work for men. The reasons for this preference were: an overly competitive boss, a boss who did not show respect or acted distrustful, or a boss who would not understand family and child care issues.

UBS™ is very similar to what "sexual harassment" was in the 1980s. It didn't happen all the time, but in instances, in which it did happen, it was denied, overlooked or treated as if the victim of it was to blame instead of the perpetrator. It also had the same effect on business.

Victims of UBS™, like those of sexual harassment are afraid to speak up due to the fact that they may be victims of retaliation, such as being written up, demoted or fired. In interviewing women for this book, most of them said that they were in too much fear of economic insecurity to speak up about their boss or co-worker. In one for instance, a woman did speak up, she was quickly warned that she had an attitude problem. In another instance, when a woman tried to speak up about her boss and gave specific examples to a human resources manager at her company, she was let go three weeks later without cause. Previously, she had a stellar record with the company and her department was thriving.

There is hope for the future for women in business, but first let's take a look at UBS™, the women who are affected by it and the women who are causing the harm and what's driving it.

Chapter Three
WHAT IS UBS™?

"Thrown under the bus" is generally defined as meaning to sacrifice, treat as a scapegoat or to betray. It's often thought of as a sudden, abrupt or brutal sacrifice of a loyal teammate, associate, co-worker, supervisor, subordinate or friend to gain a temporary advantage. In this book, the stories frequently mention female bosses or co-workers. However, during my research, I also spoke with female bosses who had subordinates or members of their staff "throw them under the bus" in order to get ahead, attempt to take their boss' position and, in a few cases, ultimately take the boss' position.

In this book, the phrase, "throwing under the bus" will be shortened to "under the bus." The throw is implied. The phenomenon of this behavior will be noted as Under the Bus Syndrome™ or UBS™.

Under the Bus Syndrome™ or UBS™
A trend in business by which a percentage of women are throwing subordinates, bosses or co-workers whom are also women under the bus. It is often sudden or abrupt but can also be chronic sacrificing, scapegoating or betraying other women at their places of business for some type of perceived or real gain.

The woman doing the throwing will lovingly be referred to at times as the UBSer™. It might be a sign they are a B.S.er and that is not an accident. It's not an endearing term but it does not imply that it's the person's nature – just a current life strategy or poor behavior.

We all may need to think we need to "bitch about the bitch," so to speak. This only brings limited and short-term relief. More long-term strategies and solutions will be explored in this book.

It is said that if you complain, you remain in the problem. The empowerment strategies contained within the solution sections will allow you to get past the identification of UBS™, the reasons why some women act out with the syndrome and how we can change it individually and collectively.

It's hard to imagine that this behavior goes on in business when in society overall, except for a select amount of sports or entertainment moms (you know who you are or "they" are), women are very kind, nurturing and supportive of each other.

As a woman in business for over 25 years, I have observed a thing or two about women in the workplace. I thought my experiences with female bosses and co-workers were unique. Typically, I want to believe the best in people and I still do. I have worked for and with some extraordinary women, but having experienced such maliciousness from a female boss, I was compelled to inquire if other women had similar experiences. After speaking with several women and observing on the job shenanigans from female bosses, coworkers and subordinates over the years, I began to see a pattern emerging.

As the women were telling their stories during my interviews and discussions, they were not speaking from a place of anger or victim hood, but from a place of shock and disappointment. Most of the interviewees initially truly liked or at least respected their bosses or co-workers. The majority of women loved their jobs and mentioned that they were generally satisfied with their job, co-workers and the companies and organizations in which they worked.

At first, most of the women had enough awareness to analyze the situation and see if their actions or attitudes were the cause of their difficulties with their female bosses or co-workers. When they tried to objectively observe or talk to a friend, partner or spouse about the situation, they also started to see a pattern emerge. They noticed attitudes, behaviors and actions on the part of their boss or co-worker that was consistently demeaning, underhanded, unkind, politically motivated, self-serving, narcissistic or contemptuous. Typically, this was at the expense of the women's self-esteem and self-confidence. The actions were often belittling or demeaning in front of other co-workers or management. The scapegoating or blaming was done in front of others so the victims of UBS™ could not counter the claims without coming across as insubordinate, jealous, overly competitive, defiant or bitchy. Highly capable and talented women were beginning to doubt themselves because of the other women who were acting against them under the influence of "UBS™".

In most cases, the women would directly ask the female bosses or co-workers who were treating them poorly if they were doing something wrong or offensive. These women initially thought they had done something that must have compelled their female bosses, co-workers or subordinates to throw them under the bus. If confronted publicly or in front of any other employee, the women with UBS™ would find a way to humiliate the women who "dare" confront them. Often, the true offenders would deny any wrongdoing on anyone's part when confronted privately. In a few cases, the egregious female boss or co-worker would state how much she hates how women treat other women in business and doesn't understand why such situations take place. The denial suggests the underlying subconscious or unconscious thoughts, feelings and behaviors that are at the heart of UBS™.

UBSer™

A woman who through insecurity, lack of internal validation or a perceived threat throws another woman under the bus. She can be a boss, subordinate or co-worker. The term sounds as if the woman doing the throwing is a bull shipper and that is not an accident. It also describes a woman who is not internally validating and is focused on "having" and "doing" regardless of the cost to other women.

It was pointed out to me by a portion of the women that they felt that the UBSer™ was fully aware of what they were doing. In one instance, the UBSer™ would remark, "I know I'm a bitch, but I get the job done." This is what Chris Liaguno, refers to as a "life strategy".

As I relayed my experience with UBS™ in the workplace, several women eagerly offered to tell their stories. Many of the women had more than one story or incident to convey. In every interview, the women did not want to tell their stories as a vengeance, vindication or for the cathartic effect it might produce. They volunteered to tell them as a way to understand the problem and find a solution. They too did not understand why women would throw other women under the bus so easily. Like me, they have many women friends and have experienced terrific female bosses and co-workers. The behaviors of the women with UBS™ seemed inexplicable.

It is not my intent to throw female bosses and coworkers who treat other woman poorly "under the bus". I truly believe that most of these women are unaware of their behavior. It has worked for them or been mimicked for them for so long that it has been hard wired into their thoughts, feelings.

I've included a pledge at the end of the book. If you would like to sign the pledge online, go to underthebusnomore.com.

Women have so much talent, greatness and intelligence to offer. Perhaps, instead of future generations of women experiencing Under the Bus Syndrome™, we can get on the bus together, peacefully and drive it to new levels of productivity, prosperity and peace. However, let's first look at the reasons for it, what's driving it and how we can individually and collectively change it.

SECTION II

Section II
REASONS, STORIES AND SOLUTIONS: TIRE TRACKS ON WOMEN'S BACKS

"You own everything that happened to you. Tell your stories. If people wanted you to write warmly about them, they should have behaved better." — Anne Lamott

As the Gloria Steinhem quote stated the truth will set you free, but first it will piss you off, these are real-life stories of UBS™. They illustrate the manifestations of the syndrome in female bosses, co-workers and subordinates and how it is not exclusive to one particular industry sector or type of business.

It has been said that through the mud and muck, the lotus flower must go before it rises above and blossoms. This is the mud and blossom section.

So, you've been thrown under the bus. Now, what do you do about it?

As you continue to read, you will see there is hope for the future. You are not alone. And as you read, my research will show what you've been through is not an isolated incident. In listening to the women tell their stories; many common themes are apparent.

We also explored and used actual solutions that have tremendously helped me and the women whom I interviewed to feel, heal and recover from their experiences with UBS™.

First the concept or reasons will be introduced. Secondly, the real-world, TireTrack

Stories that illustrate the concepts or reason why women act out in UBS™ will be reviewed. Lastly, suggested solutions will be given. Please note that the solutions discussed can be used in any of the scenarios, at any time or as part of a work/life balance routine.

WHAT'S DRIVING IT: THE SCARCITY MENTALITY

The scarcity mentality has been an infectious myth in society for hundreds of years. It is not exclusive to the United States and it is not any less common in any other countries or socio-economic communities. The scarcity mentality consists of common beliefs that were pervasive literally in every country and spanning cultures, societies and attitudes world-wide.

The three core beliefs in business are:
- **There is not enough** – in business this translates into there are not enough jobs, promotions, credit, increase, awards, increase, titles and accolades. Therefore, some will get the jobs, promotions, credit, titles, awards, incentive trips and accolades while others will get nothing or very little.
- **That's the way we've always done it or it's just the way things are** – in business this translates to helplessness, an unsolvable problem or no escape from what is going on around you. It assumes that no one is capable of changing or solving problems in the workplace or making it any better. It also signifies that there are no other options or solutions available. This attitude stifles creativity and assumes that anyone challenging the status quo is a trouble maker.
- **More is better** – in business this translates to having more means that you are more – more talented, capable, deserving. And, others around you are less. This reinforces the ego dis-ease of comparison.

During my research, I discovered that the reason women treat other women poorly in business is often due to the scarcity mentality. This is an internal belief that there is lack or not enough to go around. The thought that there are limited jobs, opportunities, accolades and the list goes on.

The other aspect of this mentality is in the continued pursuit or chase for more. It doesn't really matter what the more looks like…more money, more titles, more awards, more houses, more clothes, more shoes, more, more, more is the mantra.

No matter how much more these women attain or collect, this mentality acts as an insatiable beast compelling them onward sacrificing the females around them, their family lives, spouses/partners, children, hobbies, personal time and robbing them of any true fulfillment. When more is never enough, where does it end? It will never be enough, so the chase ensues. Their lives are full of empty conditional statements of "I'll spend more time with my kids when …" or "I'll be happy or feel fulfilled, when…"

The scarcity mentality manifests itself in three distinct ways when it comes to business and day-to-day living according to Liaguno.

1. Goal oriented versus process oriented
2. Reality is narrowly focused
3. Competition instead of cooperation

Goal Oriented versus Process Oriented

Women are conditioned from an early age to go for specific goals and focus on the results. However, often the goals are the goals of their parents, teachers and coaches. In order to survive and succeed, the steps along the way, generally speaking are not given as much importance as the end result. We have all heard the saying, "life is the journey not the destination." However, we as a society are only beginning to celebrate the process or the journey as much as we do the destination or the results.

This social conditioning is not exclusive to women. Western society is focused on instant gratification. I have had to look at my own behavior as an IGG™ or "Instant Gratification Girl™" when it comes to shopping. I have reformed but not without unlearning thoughts, emotions and behaviors and learning healthier ways of thinking, emoting, and behaving. As an instant gratification society, the quicker we can get to what we want, the better. In some cases, the need to get the

Instant Gratification Girl™ or IGG™

A woman ruled by what she wants in the moment. "I want it and I want it now" is the IGG Mantra. It's a temporary fix, sensation of relief at the expense of rational thinking, feeling, activity or reality.

desired outcome is at the expense of throwing someone under the bus. Women can get fixated on achieving or getting things as the goal. They forget about the process it takes to get there. "Often the desired results are achieved, but there is no satisfaction in attaining them and then it's on to the next one," said Maura (a former UBSer™). "I was kind of acting like a robot because I would get the incentive trips, the vacation home or the greatest cars, but I didn't really care once I got them. It was kind of maddening, "she continued.

When women get in fear over keeping their jobs, getting promoted or being recognized then they begin to see their female subordinates as a threat. How can I get mine, if you're getting yours? This is a question women subconsciously say to other women if they are acting out in UBS™.

Reality is Narrowly Focused

The scarcity mentality rears its ugly head when women do not focus on reality from a full perspective. This plays out with women thinking only in the short term in regards to their job or their status within the company. The belief about the limited amount of jobs or chance for advancement creates the mentality that women need to be extra competitive in order to succeed. This competitive nature will make women sacrifice their subordinates or co-workers for short-term gain. Instead of seeing a female subordinate's talents as an asset, many women find them to be a threat. "She's trying to take my job" or "she'll stop me from making VP" or "I am going to make her look bad, so I can get promoted instead" is the cry of females plighted by UBS™.

These women are in fear and are terribly insecure. They feel threatened when they should feel grateful for a competent staff or co-workers. Enlightened leaders in business typically have a wide view of reality. They strive to hire and promote staff members who are brighter and more talented than they are because they know it is a benefit to the company in the long term. Leaders will help their staff advance. We have all heard the term of giving a "hand up" instead of a "hand out". Leaders ensure their staff has the training, tools, and resources they need to succeed. They take a collaborative approach to business. This way all members of the team are valued and have a voice.

In the corporate world, the new economy is dictating that companies become more collaborative in nature. With the ability for everyone including customers to publish information about brands, companies, and products, there is no longer a "top down" approach to disseminating information. The hierarchical system where only the executives are informed of the inner most workings of the company are starting to evolve. Roles are shifting and many workers are being trained to have knowledge in multiple areas of the business.

Even with this evolution in business, female managers with a narrow focus on reality are often intimidated by their female staff members and will tend to hold them back or make them look bad in front of others. Despite the ability for many employees to get once considered, "top down" information with the rest of the executive team, it is not keeping these UBS™ bosses from withholding some critical tidbit that would benefit their female subordinate or co-worker from knowing. This willful omission, suppression or distorting of information is also costing companies money, time, and morale issues. These managers use this as a strategy of survival and often times, promotion. They do not care about the long-term implications that it costs the individual, team, or company. They are fixated on short-term gain.

Instead of women banding together to compete against other companies or to improve their own operational efficiencies, they are competing against one another for selfish, fearful, short-term gain. UBS™ shows itself as competition instead of cooperation. It becomes a character strategy to survive and succeed and it is reinforced and socially conditioned.

While interviewing several women for this book, they remarked how they found out after they were let go or reprimanded that their female boss or co-worker had done similar egregious acts to former or current female workers at the company. It was rarely an isolated incident.

"During the interview process, Iris kept mentioning the current marketing director in a derogatory way. I thought it was strange, but I was so excited about the prospect of a new job that I overlooked it," said Kirsten. "After working there for about eight months, I found out that she had fired two of my predecessors. Iris said a lot of nasty things about both of them to a lot of people including me. After I was fired, I felt really stupid for ignoring her trash talk," she continued.

As with most character strategies or behavior patterns, people will continue to do them until they are forced to change or have an epiphany about them.

Competition versus Cooperation

It's difficult to understand if the scarcity mentality in women with UBS™ is due to the lack of jobs in the current economy or if it is a subconscious lingering from former decades. However, it has resulted with these women, all female subordinates and co-workers, as their competition. "If there are only a few jobs or only a few management positions, then women with UBS™ think they have to be extra competitive," says Liaguno.

Being competitive in and of itself is not a problem. It can fuel great ideas and challenge people to work to the best of their abilities. Many strong leaders believe themselves to be their greatest competitor. This means that they can only improve upon themselves and they realize that their strategies vacillate between internal and external validation.

Female bosses with UBS™ do not internally validate themselves at all and do not seek external validation from their staff. They do not want to cooperate on the chance of one of their female subordinates coming up with a great idea that may lead to their promotion or reward. It's not survival of the fittest as they may delude themselves to thinking, but survival of the self-serving. Again, the strategy may work, but hopefully only in the short term.

As previously mentioned, the new economy is one of collaboration. Transparency is important for relationships of companies with their customers. It is also getting more and more important within the structures of companies themselves.

Many male executives and co-workers, unknowingly support the female bosses with UBS™ because they think they are "superstars". If many of them knew the truth, they would see that they have promoted or rewarded these women who have systematically and strategically competed with and mentally or emotionally killed the women around them who quite possibly were the most significant overall contributors to the company's success.

Here are a few questions to consider:

- Have you ever worked for a company where a female boss has consistently hired and fired several female employees for the same role while the male employees have worked for her for years?
- Have you ever been warned when you were hired that the female boss tends to be hard to work with or is a real witch?
- Have you ever been told that your role or office is cursed because the female boss doesn't keep people around for long?
- Have you been told not to decorate your office because the female boss moves people around a lot?

Surprisingly, the women who were interviewed for this book all have answered yes to one or more of the questions above.

It was apparent that many of the women were fired by their bosses with UBS™ while others decided to quit of their own accord. There must be a percentage of women in the workforce today who have bosses with UBS™ and have decided to extinguish their light and their talents so they don't appear as a threat to their female bosses or co-workers. They took themselves out of the perceived competition and therefore stopped presenting great ideas and lending their voice to the discussion. This results in a loss of productivity, innovation, profits, and low morale.

While working as an executive staffing consultant, I studied the reports and statistics on why people leave their jobs. The number one reason they leave is due to their boss. The second reason is that they feel they are not contributing.

This stands to reason that most women will not voice their opinion or ideas if they feel they are in direct competition with their immediate female supervisor. However, these women may not leave a company for personal economic reasons. The women are suffering under a female boss who consistently and competitively represses them.

The other aspect of competition may spring up at an early age when mothers and daughters seem to clash over attention from male family members or attractiveness to males outside of the family. This competition is also unhealthy and can spill over into the working world exhibiting itself in UBS™ while the mother is at work or when the daughter grows up and enters the workforce. External validation from males is highly regarded and these women will be extremely competitive in order to receive it regardless of the cost to other females around them.

Next are the real-life stories which illustrate the scarcity mentality. Following the stories are suggested solutions.

Scarcity Mentality
TIRE TRACKS: TALIA

Vanessa enjoyed her job at the non-profit organization. She had worked for almost ten years at a job that allowed her the flexibility she needed to attend to her three kids. She was the general office manager and grant writer. She knew that she had written over 40 grants and that she had earned the support and respect of many foundation directors who had provided funding to her grant requests. Vanessa had spent a good amount of her time over the years working with the foundation directors and knew most of them well.

Vanessa also had a good working relationship with the board of directors and was looking forward to the new executive director, Talia joining the team. Talia had held an executive director position at another office of the non-profit and Vanessa's division was very eager for Talia to get started. Talia started off being very cordial to everyone and observing the day-to-day operations of the office. She spent several days reviewing the grants, reports, events and volunteer activities.

Slowly and methodically, Talia began to pick apart everything that Vanessa was working on or doing. She also began to make comments about a few of the managers and their in-competencies to the other members of the staff. Initially everyone in the office thought this was just Talia's way of adjusting to a new environment. Talia would also leave for hours at a time without letting anyone know of her whereabouts.

Vanessa was in earshot of Talia one day when she overheard her complaining. "Vanessa isn't very pleasant on the phone and the language in her grants is wrong," said Talia.

Vanessa was embarrassed and mortified. Talia had never mentioned any concerns to her whatsoever nor had anyone complained to her directly about her phone voice or her grants. She decided to speak to Talia privately about her complaints. When Vanessa inquired the next day about her performance, Talia half smiled and said "you are doing just fine, Vanessa."

Vanessa said "the grant guide specifies language, formatting and documentation that needs to be provided to foundations in the grant proposal, in order for a non-profit to be considered for funding." She continued, I have been writing grants for over 10 years and know the foundation directors and what they want to see in their proposals. Talia said, "I don't know what you're talking about." "Well, said Vanessa, I overheard you talking about me to the staff yesterday." "I certainly was not talking about you, Vanessa. You are mistaken," said Talia. "She then mumbled something under her breath and walked away," said Vanessa. It was just plain awkward trying to communicate with her, Vanessa continued.

Talia took every grant proposal that Vanessa had written and marked it up extensively. "Every proposal looked like a bloody, marked up mess with red ink," said Vanessa. When Vanessa tried to tell her that she was following the specifics of the grant guide, Talia said, "these simply won't do, you don't seem to get it, you need to change them as marked, do you understand me?"

Stunned, Vanessa would make the changes and put the grants back on Talia's desk. Talia would then call Vanessa back into her office and say, "these changes make a much better proposal. Also, I am going to change your title to put it more in line with my leadership direction. Don't look at it as a demotion; it's more specific to what you do," said Talia.

Dog and Fire Hydrant

This is a case of "The Dog and Fire Hydrant"™, a term for making a mark on someone's work or information. It can be in written, digital or verbal form simply for the purpose of marking it. The purpose of the mark is to make an assertion which does not improve the work or information. This is similar to a dog peeing on a fire hydrant to get his or her scent (mark) on the hydrant, not to add anything of value to the hydrant (work).

The foundation directors who received the grant proposals would call Vanessa and complain, "What the hell? We have never seen a grant proposal like this from you before." Vanessa tried to cover for herself saying "we are taking a new approach." The non-profit did not see repeat funding support as they had in the past 10 years. The foundation directors were disillusioned and dismayed by the new approach that Talia had dictated.

The organization was awarded a substantial project that Vanessa had been working on for over one year prior to Talia's joining the team. Talia took credit for it in front of the board of directors. The board questioned Talia about the loss of grant funding from foundations. Talia incredulously said, "Vanessa, unfortunately is going through a hard time and wrote them poorly."

Vanessa's co-worker Renee mentioned to Vanessa that Talia was speaking ill of her. "She told us that you were sounding unprofessional on the phone and that your work was subpar," said Renee. She, also, mentioned that she was going to be hiring a new person to help us with the work load. Renee said that she told Talia that it was not really her business and that Talia should speak to Vanessa directly if she had concerns.

Vanessa asked to have a meeting with Talia as she was in complete shock. Previously, she had great reviews, been awarded grants, been awarded the recent project and got along with everyone in the organization. She, also, was told that she had a pleasant phone voice.

At the meeting, Vanessa said "I've heard that you have some concerns about me. How am I doing from your perspective?" Talia said "well, Vanessa, I think you are doing great. Why do you ask?" Vanessa continued, "A few of the employees have said that you are not happy with my performance". Talia retorted, "You do seem a bit stressed and I want to ease that burden so I'm hiring a new employee and she starts Monday".

Vanessa initially believed that Talia hired Nancy to help. However, the second week Nancy was on the job, she cut her hair in the same style as Talia. Vanessa, as well as others, could hear Nancy complaining about Vanessa to Talia. When Vanessa asked Nancy about her complaints, Nancy said," I wouldn't do that, I hate when women are mean to other women in business". The pressure became too much for Vanessa so she decided to resign. The members of the board were saddened to see Vanessa go, but they did not want to rock the boat with Talia. At the time of the resignation, Talia had tried to convince Vanessa that it was a mutual departure or that the organization fired Vanessa. Talia immediately announced that Nancy was hired as a replacement for Vanessa. Six months after Vanessa's departure, Talia was still trying to blame Vanessa for various challenges around the office.

"I was glad that I resigned before Talia could completely throw me under the bus," said Vanessa. She continued, "I know I was dedicated to the success of that non-profit". Talia was completely dedicated to her own agenda. And, that's dangerous.

You can continue to read two other Scarcity Mentality Tire Tracks or skip to the Solutions section.

Scarcity Mentality
TIRE TRACKS: LIZ

Carla worked in the school district for about ten years as an ESL (English as a Second Language) Specialist. She loved her boss and her job. She prided herself in ensuring that her students received the best education possible. Her boss, Monica was one of the best bosses she had ever experienced. Monica made it her mission to get to know her staff. She knew each teacher's strengths and talents. Monica would bring opportunities to her staff to continue their education or to promote them even if that meant they no longer worked in her department. She welcomed open communication and she tried to lift up everyone around her.

Monica was offered a promotion to work at another school district. Carla was saddened by the news. Her sadness was tempered by the fact that Monica had trained her replacement, Liz. Initially, Carla was very hopeful for the division because Monica was so wonderful.

For a couple of years, everything ran smoothly because the duties of the division were split between Anna and Liz. Carla had very little contact with Liz. Anna made most of the major decisions as unlike Liz, Anna had worked in education for the majority of her career.

Anna had to leave for personal reasons and Liz took over the division and all its responsibilities. "All of sudden decisions were made in a frantic, impetuous manner," said Carla.

Carla continued that Liz acted like she didn't trust anyone and did not share her vision for the division, if she had one. "Liz did not care about my development and never spoke to me about additional education or opportunities. She was the polar opposite of Monica," said Carla.

Carla thought that maybe Liz had never had so much responsibility before in a job and decided to excuse her behavior as being a "newbee". She was also encouraged because Liz insisted that the entire staff of ESL Specialists go to a four-day workshop on how to facilitate effective meetings and conduct business. Carla was very excited about the workshop. She believed that Liz was aware of how dysfunctional the staff meetings were conducted. Carla said, 'there was no inherent trust of the staff by Liz as there was by Monica or Anna. We felt Liz was against us and now, we felt pleasantly surprised that she was trying to bring us together through attending this workshop."

The excitement from the staff was short lived. After the workshop, Liz would not allow the meetings to be co-facilitated and no one was allowed to share. "Liz was ill prepared for the meetings and was not receptive to hearing from anyone who was trying to make them productive. Liz sent out an email one week after our last meeting stating that the meetings were not productive and were being disbanded altogether for the rest of the school year," said Carla. During all her years as an educator, Carla had never known a boss who did not have regular staff meetings with the teachers.

At the beginning of the next school year, Liz sent out a notice for a meeting. During this meeting, she changed the roles in the department and issued three directives that everyone would need to follow.

Approximately two weeks prior to the meeting, Carla let Liz know that she would be late for the meeting due to a prior commitment. Carla also requested to be brought up to speed after the meeting by Liz or have the directives sent to her via email. Liz did not respond.

Liz conducted the meeting and acted put out when Carla arrived late. Liz said in front of the entire staff, "Because you're late Carla, here's your role." Carla was surprised. "Liz did not reiterate what the three directives were during the rest of the meeting" said Carla. Liz was not available after the meeting to make additional inquiries. She failed to email the directives to me despite my prior request. One week later, Carla was called into Liz's office. "She proceeded to reprimand me for not following the directives in my job," said Carla.

"After 10 years of receiving high marks and accolades for my work, I was being reprimanded like a naughty puppy," said Carla. She continued Liz asked Tina to be present during my reprimand. Tina was responsible to evaluate my performance and would later be one of my supervisors.

I asked Liz to please review the three directives because they were never communicated to me despite my requests for the information. Liz gave me a dirty look and said, "We don't want to see you in this office for two weeks."

Before I left Liz's office, "I asked Liz why aren't we providing specific materials and information to the teachers and students at the beginning of this school year like we were providing to them for the last ten years?," said Carla. Liz shot Carla a look as if she wanted to hurt her.

Carla continued, "Liz was giving her looks and getting angry because I was raising issues about standards in education. Liz did not have much experience in secondary education. Instead of collaborating with me regarding what was needed for the division, Liz would get upset."

Carla was trying to get Liz to look at what was the best possible ESL curriculum for the teachers and students. Carla was not trying to make Liz look uninformed or knowledgeable. Liz did not appear to be interested in what was best for the students or the teachers. She had her own agenda.

A couple days after the reprimand, Liz came into Carla's office, threw the materials on her desk and said, "you want standards – here order all this stuff yourself." Carla was shocked. She honestly wanted to help Liz, not make her angry. She had never been asked to order the materials as Monica or Anna always ordered the materials at the beginning of the school year as part of their role.

When Carla met with Tina for her performance review, she was very disappointed for two reasons. First, it was the lowest marks she had ever received. For 10 years, she had received excellent marks and this year she was deemed "adequate".

Second, she was told by Liz to not communicate or speak up on what the division staff needed. Tina reprimanded her in the evaluation stating that she continues to withhold information that could be useful for the division by not speaking up on what is needed.

Although Carla continues to work for Liz, she is very guarded. She does not make requests or offer suggestions because she fears retaliation and reprisal. She also knows that she most likely is compromising her and the division's and the students' educational standards in order to keep her job.

You can continue to read one other Scarcity Mentality Tire Tracks or skip to the Solutions section.

Scarcity Mentality
TIRE TRACKS: JENNIFER

Alex loved her job at the department store. She worked there for over five years and was steadily making her numbers and getting a lot of kudos from the patrons of the store as well as her fellow employees and management. She had a terrific working relationship with her boss, Marietta. Alex knew that Marietta was fair but firm and she always told Alex that she thought Alex was an excellent employee.

Alex became friends with many of her co-workers. They would often go to happy hour after their shift on Fridays and would meet up on their off hours to do various activities. "The trouble started when I began to confide in some of the women, especially my co-worker, Jennifer," said Alex. "Our store was one of the best performing stores in the region and the entire state. Many of our top executives were being promoted while others were asked to stay where they were because they were doing such a great job," she continued. Alex remarked that many of the sales associates were also asked to keep up the good work and I questioned if I would ever be promoted.

"Although I loved my job, I decided to interview elsewhere because my pay was capped and I just wanted to see what my options might be," said Alex. "I thought Jennifer was a close-mouthed friend at the time and I mentioned to her that I was curious and decided to interview for a flight attendant position with a major airline carrier," she continued. "I truly loved my retail job and wasn't seriously looking elsewhere, "said Alex. "I also thought Jennifer was a dear friend and felt comfortable telling her anything," said Alex.

Marietta was promoted to be a manager of a new store that was opening in another state. She called Alex into her office to tell her the news. Marietta told Alex with tears in her eyes that she was considering her and Jennifer as her replacement. Marietta said that she truly thought Alex would be a great manager but in all fairness, both she and Jennifer would be interviewed for the job.

"My heart was racing, I couldn't believe the news. This was something that I had hoped for but not under the circumstances. I would have never applied nor interviewed with the airline had I known I was being considered for the manager position, "said Alex.

"The day of the interview, I felt very confident. I knew that Marietta told everyone about me and that she was an advocate of me and my career with the company. I was to interview last as I had to work the floor earlier in the morning since we were running a big sale that would run through the weekend," said Alex.

She continued "as I walked down the hallway for my interview, I saw Jennifer coming out of the conference room. She smiled at me in a very fake way where her lips went up into a semi-circle and then quickly dropped dismissively and I began to feel a little nervous. When I came into the conference room, Marietta shook my hand but she too did not greet me with her usual warm smile. The interview did not go as well as I had hoped. I couldn't put my finger on it at the time, but I felt that I was no longer being considered and that the management team had already made up their mind."

"I tried calling Jennifer later in the evening, but it rang and went directly to voicemail. I had a weird feeling in my gut" said Alex. I worked the weekend shift but did not run into Jennifer or hear back from her. When I went into work the following Tuesday, Rebecca, another co-worker asked if I had heard the good news. "What are you referring to, Rebecca?" I asked. "Jennifer got Marietta's job," said Rebecca. "I was in shock and ran to the restroom with tears in my eyes," said Alex. I wondered how Jennifer was picked over me. After I choked back my tears and fixed my makeup, I walked calmly over to Rebecca. "I was really hoping to get that job. It's a perfect fit for me," I said.

"Well, we all thought so too, but Jennifer told Marietta and the others in the interview that you were interviewing with an airline because you didn't really like working retail," said Rebecca. "I was stunned," said Alex. "I was foolish to have trusted Jennifer, but I never thought in a million years, she would twist the information so she could get ahead," said Alex.

Scarcity Mentality
SUGGESTED SOLUTIONS

"We forgive, then, out of self-interest. I forgive you because I want out of my pain. I forgive you so that I can be free of what you did. I see beyond your mistake to the love in you so that I can see beyond the mistake to the love in me---because only then can I have a miracle." — Marianne Williamson

It's difficult to look beyond our current circumstances and our anger when we have been affected by someone with UBS™. It's equally difficult to be aware of the fact that we are hurting another due to the fact we are suffering from UBS™.

We'll explore several options to overcome, avoid or recover quickly from the effects of UBS. It's very common to be caught up in self-pity, obsessive thoughts, and negativity. It's also easy to want justice, revenge, or some other act of anger against someone who hurts your pride, ego, or livelihood. As with most situations, the one creating the pain is most likely hurting themselves in some way. Hurting people tend to hurt people to temporarily relieve their pain.

When faced with a situation where another female is making your work life miserable, there are basically four options available to you.
1. Stay and be miserable
2. Leave the company
3. Go to human resources or an up-line supervisor about it
4. Change yourself

Unfortunately, jobs are not as plentiful as they used to be in many industry sectors. Due to economic reasons, family obligations, retirement plans, and other commitments most women cannot quit their jobs or their current company.

Opportunities to forge ahead on your own with new and different ideas for emerging companies, small businesses or starting your own company are limitless. However, if you are under the influence of an UBSer™, chances are you no longer have the confidence or drive to make that type of leap of faith to leave your current situation. It feels risky because you're not centered, internally validating, or trusting in your faith. You believe and perhaps, buy into the bad press the UBSer™ has told you directly or distributed about you amongst your peers, associates, and management.

Another fear may be in approaching human resources or up-line management. In many companies these people can help in addressing the issues you are facing with the UBSer™. In other instances, and through my interviews with women, the HR representatives and up-line supervisors have been instrumental in getting the victims of the UBSer™ written up as insubordinate, a trouble maker, or emotionally or professionally unstable.

In a high percentage of the cases, the women were laid off or fired. It did not matter which approach they took in speaking about the incident or incidences of being thrown under the bus. Nor did it matter if the behaviors of the UBSers™ affected the employee relaying the information, department, company morale, or the bottom line. Several of the interviewees of this book were forced to sign documents that indemnify the companies from any wrongdoing and against litigation. This might be the single greatest reason that changing yourself might be the best option.

This is not to say that you aren't a talented and skilled professional. The reasoning is that you might be able to change jobs, move to another department, or get hired at another company. However, unless you are willing to change yourself, the situation most likely will present itself again with another UBSer™ repeatedly victimizing you. Aren't you a little tired of the BS and the UBSers™?

A Word to The Why's

You've been laid off, fired, put on suspension, warned, threatened, gossiped about or basically, thrown under the bus. Now, what do you do?

Under the Solutions Sections, you will see there is hope for the future. I was not alone in my experience. You are not alone, either. As my research has shown this is not an isolated incident – what just happened to you or has happened to you. In listening to the women tell their stories; many common themes were apparent. Just as frequently we discussed how they were able to heal and recover from what happened. They as well as I have used many methods and strategies to feel confident, empowered and content with our work lives. And you can too.

First, it's best not to get caught up in the questions such as: why me? Why now? Why did she do that? Why was I ignored, passed over or sabotaged? A word to the whys – stop. Once you've evaluated your part in the whole scenario, a better question is what's next or where do I go from here?

Not-so Zen Koan
What is the sound of one bitch slapping?

You may never be able to answer why. It's a not-so-Zen koan – what is the sound of one bitch slapping™? No one really knows the answer. Let's look at suggestions that have truly helped women to feel confident, empowered and content.

Journaling – The Road Ahead
When I was thrown under the bus, I began to write. I wrote down everything that happened to me and how it made me feel. I had so many questions running through my head because I was shocked. I wrote it on my laptop putting down anything and everything that came to mind.

A week later, I reread what I had written. This time, I was logical and separated from my initial emotions. It helped me to see what if anything was my part and what I needed to do next.

It made me realize that I needed to start/continue practicing the solutions that are suggested in this book.

If you are experiencing an UBSer™ or have recently been thrown under the bus, I suggest you write about it. Here are a few questions that you may wish to consider once you've written what happened and how it made you feel.
- Do I need to seek legal counsel or speak with human resources?
- Am I reliving the scenario over and over again obsessively? If so, where can I get psychological or emotional help or support? Do we have an Employee Assistance Program? Or if you were let go, where can I get mental health support at a reasonable cost?
- Where can I get job seeking or career placement assistance or get a coach?
- Do I need to contact Human Resources to understand when my medical, retirement and savings benefits are over? Do I need to ask for contact information for any plans that will continue past working for this company?
- Where do I go from here?

The solutions suggested throughout this book are ones to assist you when you've been thrown under the bus. The solutions are also a means to assist in the changing of UBS™, the effects of it and to empower you toward a brighter future.

Positive Affirmations

"I'm good enough, I'm smart enough and gosh darn it, people like me."
— *Character: Stewart Smalley/SNL Skit*

One of the most fundamental ways to create change in your life is to change your thinking. Having experienced an UBSer™, you might feel that you have begun to give yourself a lot of negative self-talk. Your thinking may be skewed by what the UBSer™ said or what you believe she inferred about you. It might seem easier to begin to believe these lies and tell yourself that you're not good enough, smart enough, too old, too inexperienced, or not caught up on the latest technology.

If this type of thinking persists for too long, you'll eventually let it define you and stop yourself from fulfilling your purpose. Setbacks, job loss, self-esteem loss are what happened to you. They are not who you are or not indicative of the greatness that you can become.

"As a man believeth, so he is." Or with all due respect, "As a woman believeth, so she is."
— *Matthew*

Before we start the part on positive affirmations, let's examine denial. When I'm referring to denial, it's denial of what your UBSer said about you. I'm talking about being in denial that the situation or the words used against you are a reflection of your authentic self.

Examples of declarations of denial to help move you forward:
- My UBSer™ words are untrue, I am capable, talented and equipped.
- My UBSer™ has no power over me; I am what God says I am.

One of my favorites is from my mentor, Dr. Debra Wingfield:
I release the messages from my UBSer™ and step into my personal power.

Use the actual facts as you know them about yourself and avoid being pulled back into the blaming and denial of the UBSer™. It is highly likely that you are no longer in denial. She is responsible for her behavior toward you.

It is here that the part of the serenity prayer comes into play – acceptance of the things you cannot change, courage to change the things you can and the wisdom to know the difference. In the meantime, continual use of positive affirmations will also aid in personal changes and growth. Let's explore those further.

We've all heard or seen positive affirmations but we often have forgotten to use them in our daily lives. Many athletes and entertainers utilize both visioning and positive affirmations to help them perform at their highest levels. We can utilize them as a strategy to keep ourselves focused, positive, uplifted, and on-track.

When you are experiencing an UBSer™ or stress of any kind, turning to methods of meditation, relaxation, and positive affirmation can help to put your mind at peace or to focus your energy and efforts.

It has been said by many religious and spiritual teachers that if you want to change your life, change your thinking. Our thoughts are powerful. If you don't believe it, test it out for yourself.

If what we think about expands – again, I request that you test it out. We have all heard about professional athletes who have consistently thought about winning a competition and then doing so. We have, also, heard of people who have been so focused on becoming or being ill that they have actually manifested illness or "dis-ease".

You might be thinking that the movie and books sound great but "I'm reading this book right now." I learned much about positive affirmations from books and programs from professional coaches, spiritual advisors, and mentors. I also spoke to countless friends and acquaintances who felt that positive thinking (coupled with feelings and action at times) brought about positive results in their lives. I experimented with the concept and experienced positive results as well.

I request that you try positive affirmations as an experiment in your life and see how it works. Plus, by its very nature, it can benefit your mood and others around you.

Granted, it's important to be authentic in all you do and say as often as you can. After all, you have experienced an UBSer™ or you are a reformed UBSer™ and working with or as a person who throws people under the bus is no picnic.

In the beginning, you might have to "fake it, 'til you make it" as it is said in many recovery programs. The point is to make a beginning as soon as you can and to try to say the positive affirmations for at least 30 days and see if you are experiencing any favorable changes.

Those of you who are of a religious or spiritual nature may also have heard of speaking favor over your lives. Where you said words or gave thanks for positive things occurring in your life prior to their coming to fruition.

Before we start to review sample affirmations, here are a few methods to use in saying them – either out loud or silently in your own mind. (These are listed in no particular order because it doesn't matter which method you pick as long as you pick one or two that resonate with you.)

1. While walking, running or exercising.
2. Write the affirmations on index cards and say them upon awakening and right before you go to sleep.
3. Get a set of beads and say an affirmation per bead until you've made a complete rotation through the beaded necklace or bracelet. Try this on a daily basis at the same time each day for 30 days.
4. Say the affirmations throughout the day whenever you remember.
5. Put sticky notes or tape notes around your house with various affirmations on them.
6. Put notes on your bathroom mirror with affirmations on them and say them whenever you go to the bathroom. Who cares if your company thinks you're nuts? This is your journey.
7. Have your favorite affirmation engraved on a mirror. One of my dearest friends received an affirmation engraved on a small mirror. She reads it every day while she puts on her makeup. She is a very positive person, hmmm.

Here are examples of affirmations that I use and the women I interviewed use on a daily basis. Choose any of them that might resonate with you or write your own.

- *I am talented, capable and equipped. I can do what I set my mind to do.*
- *I am healthy, happy and prosperous.*
- *I am happy and grateful that great things always come my way.*
- *I am happy and grateful that I attract the right people, resources and opportunities.*

You can add your favorites. An important part in using affirmations is to repeat them regularly and be thankful for them as if they have already come to pass. Watch for negative or doubtful thoughts to enter your mind. Develop your method for saying them, believing them to be true and then let them go as if you are giving them up to God or the universe in anticipation of the magic to happen.

Of course, there may not be immediate change. However, over time, you will most likely observe many positive changes in your life. At the very least, your experience of the UBSer™ will feel a little less overwhelming and you will feel more at peace with yourself.

I affirm and know that you the reader are going to experience a more positive outlook for your life and that favor and increase are coming your way. And, so it is.

Friends Along the Road

"Oh, I get by from a little help from my friends." – Lyrics by the Beatles

One of the exercises that I request my coaching clients do when they are experiencing the habit of negative self-talk is to make a Three to Five Request™ of their friends.

The Three to Five Request™ is as follows:

Example 1:
- Ask at least three to five friends to email or message you with three to five things/qualities/actions/states of being they really like or love about you
- Of course, if you have more people to make the request and people want to list more than three to five items, by all means let it be

Print out or write down or carry on an electronic device these positive messages with you everywhere you go. When you are feeling down or starting with the negative self-talk, look at them.

You can also turn them into positive affirmations or a gratitude list. This will help you see what an amazing person you are and help you move forward past your negative experience.

The Three to Five Request™ is as follows:

Example 2:
Buy a journal or create an online journal.
- Every day – either in the morning or at night, write three to five things/qualities/people/pets/actions/resources/opportunities/states of being that you are grateful for and read them out loud.
- Of course, you can list as many things that you can think of that you are grateful for and they can be the same things everyday

Both examples are a means to create more positive thoughts and feelings. They are ways to assist in becoming more internally validating. And, to help you realize that the people, who matter most to you (including you) can see you for whom you really are – amazing.

Transforming Thoughts and Judgments
"Free your mind, the rest will follow" – Lyrics by Destiny's Child

This method can be used at any time when you are making a judgment on another person especially someone who has harmed you or having a lot of negative self-talk. It can help restore you to a more peaceful place if practiced often.

How it works:
Whenever you feel any judgment coming in the mind, change your breathing pattern. Immediately, you will see that the thought has disappeared.

Whenever you want to change a thought in your mind that has become a habit, breathing is the best method to make the change. All habits of the mind are associated with the pattern of breathing. Try changing the pattern of your breathing. The thoughts change immediately.

Whenever you see the judgment is coming and you are getting into an old judgment, immediately exhale – as if you are throwing the thought out when you exhale. Exhale deeply as you throw out the air, feel, visualize, that the whole judgment is being thrown out.

Then take in a deep breath, two or three times and just see what happens. So start by exhaling. When you want to take something in, start inhaling; if you want to throw something out, start by exhaling and just see how immediately the mind is affected.

Simply do this and immediately you will see that the mind has moved somewhere else. You are now in the new thinking and you will refrain from making the old judgement. This can become a very important practice for inner change.

The Prayer Bus

"Forgiveness does not mean ignoring what has been done or putting a false label on an evil act no longer remains as a barrier to the relationship. Forgiveness is a catalyst creating the atmosphere necessary for a fresh start and a new beginning." — Martin Luther King Jr

These are two very powerful suggestions that helped me and several women interviewed for this book to release the anger that was carried towards the UBSer™.

Yes, my first instinct as was that of many other women was for retaliation. It is said that hurting people, hurt people. I knew that hurting the UBSer™ would only hurt me in the end. There had to be an easier and softer way to relieve my anger. There is a saying that harboring resentment is like drinking poison and expecting the other person to die. I asked myself, how can I rid myself of my resentment against the UBSer™?

The answer came in the form of prayer.

Suggestion One:
Pray for everything that you want for yourself – health, happiness, prosperity for the woman who harmed you or is continuing to harm you. It was suggested to do this even if I didn't believe in it, even if I really didn't even want that for her and even if I had ill feelings about her. I was told to do this for a period of two weeks. Although, I have prayed my whole life, I found this difficult at first. I also prayed for God to change my heart.

"After the two week period, my heart had completely changed. It became easier and easier for me to pray for her as the days passed. I felt as if I meant it and the prayers were genuine. My feeling of anger had diminished to a level where it barely existed," said Lynn.

Suggestion Two:
There was a time when someone had incredibly hurt a family member. I was having difficulty praying for this person as in Suggestion One. In a conversation with two friends, I discovered how they each were suffering by someone who had harmed their families. I asked them for the first names of the people who had harmed their

families. We agreed to pray for the other people who had harmed each other's families for a period of two weeks. At the end of the two weeks, we met and discussed our experiences. While we each shared our experiences, we noticed that we no longer harbored any anger or resentment toward the person that had harmed our own families. It changed our hearts too. It was a tremendously freeing experience.

If you don't have friends that have had similar experiences, why not put the UBSer™ on a prayer list at your church or one on-line if you don't have a church, synagogue, center or other place of worship or meditation.

Meditation

Meditation has been practiced for thousands of years. It has been referred to as a practice, no-mind space, a method of relaxation, focusing or centering, a form of prayer, being in the zone or connecting with source. In other words, meditation is a way to remember who you really are.

When we act in UBS™ or are victims of an UBSer™, we tend to forget who we are. Our vision for ourselves gets cloudy and we need to "be still and know" that we can return to ourselves at any time.

If we look at an holistic or total approach we have to incorporate techniques not only for the mind but for the body and feelings. There are in-depth methods involved with meditation, and we will cover a few basic techniques to help empower and refocus your energy. The most common response as to why people don't meditate is, "I don't think I'm doing it right because my mind wanders." I have been meditating for over 16 years and my mind sometimes wanders too. That is why it's called a practice. It was suggested to me to go and sit with people who have been meditating for years. While sitting with other meditators, I found that I could go deeper faster. I didn't learn tennis by only trying to hit tennis balls on one occasion, so I decided to practice meditation over time as well.

Meditation can take many forms, too many to mention here. Running, dancing, and laughing can all be forms of meditation. Instead of reviewing these in depth, let's look at a few methods.

Below is a simple way to begin meditating that you can practice at home in a quiet space in your living room or any other room that is free from distractions. It's best if you can go to a room where no one else is and turn off any electronic devices or leave them in another room. Turn off the lights. If at night or if it is dark in your home, you may wish to light a candle or use a flameless candle to create a peaceful atmosphere. You can turn on music that is quiet and gentle at a low volume, but do not put in earphones. You may wish to not have any music at all.

Read through the following first, before you try to do it because it requires you closing your eyes. If you can have your eyes closed and can still read this, please contact me, I am curious to how you accomplished that skill.

Sit in a simple cross-legged position on the floor and use your hands to make sure that you are sitting up straight. If you have a bad back or one that would feel strained sitting on the floor in a cross legged position, then sit against a wall or sofa or sit in a chair with your feet on the ground.

It does not matter if you are completely comfortable as you do not have to sit here for a long period of time. Slowly, close your eyes and begin to focus on your breath. Begin to breathe in and out through your nose, continue to do this for several breaths. If it helps, you can count breathing in – one, two three, and breathing out – one, two, three. Your belly may rise and fall while you're breathing in deep breaths. Even if you start to worry if you're doing it right, just keep breathing. When you sit there, your thoughts might wander thinking about your day, your grocery list, what happened at work, your kid's soccer practice or any other thought. Don't focus on any one thought, just let it come and go. At first, you might start to feel sadness or anger or other emotions. That is normal too. Stay focused on what you are experiencing but don't let yourself get so relaxed that you begin to sleep. If you get really sleepy, it's okay to wake yourself up and turn on the lights and continue with your day or evening.

Try to sit and meditate for at least ten minutes per day at first. When you get used to it, you may try longer intervals. If you would like to use mantras or singing while you meditate that is okay to do as well. Some people prefer to read something before they meditate which really causes one to contemplate more than just experience.

As part of a past board of directors' member for a meditation group, I remember how we began our business meetings. It was one of the most centering and effective methods of getting a group of people to focus before they began discussions on operating a non-profit.

We would begin by using a timer with ten minutes of gibberish (basically making sounds that didn't mean anything and not using any recognizable words in any language) and then we would sit in meditative silence for ten minutes. When the discussions began we were all relaxed, focused, and ready for business.

I have been a meditation practitioner for over 15 years and it has been an invaluable resource in teaching me that I can return to that space of centering and calmness at any time as it is always available to me as it is always available to you. Again, there are many methods, so explore what resonates with you.

Relaxation

Reading a section about relaxation might seem silly to some people. Most of us know how to relax, right? Wrong. So often we are caught in our daily responsibilities, dealing with the stresses from many aspects in life, it stands to reason that many of us don't know how to relax. I've heard many of my women friends tell me that they are afraid to relax. "If I don't worry about things, I'm afraid something really bad will happen," one of my closest friends said to me.

Years ago, I told a friend, "things are going so well that I'm waiting for the other shoe to drop." She replied, "I'm here to tell you, there is no shoe – stop worrying."

If you have UBS™, have experienced it, or are currently experiencing it from another female in your life, chances are you can't relax easily. Reading this might be getting your heart racing or your mind wandering. Relax…yeah right.

Well, finding ways to relax and de-stress is easier that you might think. There are many ways to relax. There are many low or no cost ways to relax and there are ways that will cost some money. However, peace of mind may be worth it because you can't put a price tag on it.

Here are a few ways to relax that may be beneficial to you.
- Listening to calm music or music that makes you happy. Listening to sounds of nature such as water from a stream or ocean waves are soothing. Yes, it may make you want to pee but it's relaxing just the same.
- Taking a walk outside (if weather permits) – listening to the sounds around you – try to pay attention to all the wonderful sensory experiences around you – the sun on your face, the gentle breeze on your skin, the birds, the scenery, the fragrance
- Taking a vacation without your electronic devices with you constantly or at least plan times when they are off and out of site
- Meditation (see former section) yoga, stretching
- Working on artistic endeavors – photography, writing, playing or watching sports, painting, scrapbooking, crocheting, cooking, playing an instrument, singing, dancing – anything that makes your heart happy

- Taking deep breaths and closing your eyes – remembering the most peaceful place that you experienced. Remembering all the sensory experiences – sounds, sites, feelings, fragrance
- Reading a book purely for entertainment reasons – not studying it for college or work
- Watching a movie or television show that is purely entertaining
- Going to events that are entertaining only – not always ones that you have to for work, provide support, volunteer, make something or do something – just for enjoyment
- Going to your place of worship or spiritual affiliation

A Vision For You

"Your vision will become clear only when you can look into your own heart. Who looks outside, dreams. Who looks inside, awakes." – Carl Jung

During the interviews for this book, I informally surveyed the women to ask them if they had any visions for their lives as a child. Most of them said they did not have any specific visions or knew of visioning. Literally every one of them mentioned a vision of their wedding day. There were about one fourth of them who knew what type of profession they wanted to pursue. The roles they envisioned as children were typically considered feminine, or nurturing and supportive.

There were no strong women business leaders to emulate for those who grew up in the 60s, 70s and 80s. The male business leaders were the people that most women would try to emulate. The majority of women did not have the visioning, commitment, confidence, and strategy setting to be successful in business without utilizing or mimicking the characteristics that men use to be successful in the business environment.

As in anything in life, if you are not acting true to yourself, the results of your thoughts and actions are not optimal and often inappropriate. The techniques are a suggestion of one method of visioning. There are many techniques and you may wish to get with a life or business coach, career counselor, mentor, or your respective spiritual or religious clergy to look at visioning, commitment, accountability, and guidance.

As the times have changed, more and more women are being hired to the highest ranks of business and embracing their feminine qualities and realizing that there is room for a broad spectrum of relating and flourishing in business. When women set a vision for themselves and embrace their feminine as well as masculine qualities, there is no limit to what they can do.

How does someone go about creating a vision? You might think that it's too late in your career or you're too young or confused to know what your vision might be. You might think that you don't exhibit UBS™ and this vision creating business is only for those who do.

You might have UBS™ and think that this vision business is a waste of time and you're too busy chasing more, more, more to stop and think about a vision. How dare I, as the author of this book, take you away from the possibility of the promotion or going away on another vacation, while your nanny is raising your kids back home, where you are constantly connected to work and consider passing out at the beach from exhaustion is your idea of relaxing.

Create a Vision for You
"To thine own self be true." — the character, Polonius from Hamlet by William Shakespeare

As a life and business coach as well as a woman in business, I know that any visions or goals that you explore should have personal meaning to you. If they do, you will pursue them with a renewed energy regardless if you are new to business, are in the middle of your career or are looking to retire or reinvent yourself. As we begin this section, look within your own heart and dreams – not what your parents, spouses, partners, relatives, or friends think you should do. Yes, you can seek their input, but be true to yourself. If you are going to feel empowered, you are first person who needs to ignite your own inner fire.

Whether you feel that you have experienced UBS™ or might feel that you are a perpetrator of this syndrome, the only way to change the situation is to redefine it, change it, or enhance it. Most women or more accurately, most little girls do not sit down and map out a vision for themselves and their lives. They don't direct their energies or are taught to direct their energies as to what it is that they want out of life. What an ideal life would be for them. What does it look like? What are the emotions surrounding it? How does it feel in your body and mind?

Here is a methodology in creating a vision for you and your life. Please read this section over at least once before beginning as most of us cannot close our eyes and continue to read something. Again, read over it first before you attempt to do the visualization sequence. It might be a good idea to record it first on your Smartphone or other device so that you can experience it fully without having to break up your visualizations.

1. Set aside an hour or two on the weekend or at night. Begin by sitting quietly in your home in a place that has few distractions. Turn off your electronic equipment. Close your eyes. Slow your breathing by taking deep breaths. Imagine yourself being in the most beautiful place you have ever seen, let your senses hear the sounds around you, feel the breeze, feel the sun on your skin, feel the earth beneath you, your body and mind are very relaxed. Begin to gently ask yourself the following questions. [It's best to have a notebook (paper) and pen, laptop or tablet near where you are sitting so you can take notes about your experiences, thoughts and feelings. Yes, I know I said turn off the electronic equipment – this is for note taking purposes only.]

After about ten minutes, open your eyes and while focusing on the beautiful place in your mind begin to ask yourself these questions:

1. What does it feel like to be doing what it is that I truly love?

2. What makes my heart happy? What makes me feel at peace? What gives me a sense of satisfaction?

3. How do I want to be? What do I want to be? What did I love doing as a child? If you're a very young person – what do I love doing now?

4. Complete the following statements:

    I feel most happy when. . . . .
    I am most at peace when. . .
    I am true to myself when. . . . .

5. This next step goes a little deeper. You can go there right away from the previous steps or you can plan another time to become very still. Close your eyes again.

6. Visualize yourself going to a location that makes you feel completely calm and relaxed. Is it by the ocean, a meadow of flowers and tall grass, walking in the desert, by a lake or stream or is it high up in the mountains? Picture yourself there. What does it feel like to your senses? What do you see, hear, taste, feel, or experience in that space for 10 to 15 minutes. Know that you are safe, relaxed, and calm.

7. Imagine you sitting, lying down, or standing in this wonderful place. Your body is completely relaxed. You close your eyes and begin to feel a warm golden or white light starting at your toes then slowly moving past your

ankles to your legs. This light continues to travel upward to your pelvis and fills your abdomen. It moves at the same time in your hands and up your arms. The light continues up your body filling you with warm, relaxing, and supportive light. It travels to the top of your head. Stay there for a few minutes feeling completely energized and supported.

8. Place your hands over your eyes for a few minutes. Gently, open your eyes and feel yourself back in the room where you are reading this book. Take a few minutes to feel your body – move your feet, sway back and forth, and do light stretching.

9. Ask yourself the following question:
   - *What is it that I really love doing? (There can be multiple answers)*

10a. Write down your answers. You have now completed this exercise.

10b. If an answer or answers don't come to you, don't be discouraged. You have posed the question, so pay attention to your dreams or any ideas that come to mind over the next week or two. Write them down when they do.

After completing this exercise, you will probably be curious about what to do with the information.

Dream bigger than what you think is possible

Once you have answered some of the questions from the previous section, you probably have a pretty good idea of what your vision is about.

Whether it's going back to school to get your Masters or PhD, traveling the world helping on natural disasters, writing a best-selling book, or starting your own business, dream BIG.

Imagine what it feels like when you are living your vision. When you start to think bigger, then you begin to get ideas from everywhere on how your vision can take shape, your subconscious mind will help you.

Begin to notice the things that are beginning to come into your field of awareness that you can take action on. Notice anything that aligns with your vision. You will also begin to notice that the petty things at the office are not getting to you as much or reliving your leaving the company does not occupy your thoughts.

The important aspect of visioning is that you can create new visions for your life at any time in your career or your life. You can imagine your life as grand and expansive as you would like it to be.

Create Images, Words, and Feelings to Your Vision

Once you've determined what you would like to experience and achieve in your life, getting pictorial representation of it is the next step. You can find several free images on the Internet, in magazines and from your own photo collection that can represent your vision. Putting these images on a poster board, taping them to your mirror or placing them near your computer is a good way to make an impression on your mind. Along with the images, you might want to use words such as successful business, financially free, abundance of friends, happy home life and any other words that create a feeling of peace or align with your vision.

When you look at the images and words, always imagine what it will feel like when you achieve it. Think of yourself as already being where your vision says you're going. It is suggested to do this several times per day. This exercise will help you to focus on the road ahead.

List It

Another suggestion for creating a job you love is to write down a list of everything you want in your next job or perhaps your current job. For example:

1. My talents and skills are valued
2. The people are supportive, professional, intelligent and forward thinking
3. I can contribute and I'm compensated well for it
4. I can learn, grow and feel a part of an organization who not only provides great products and services but has initiatives to serve my community and the world

These are a few examples. It is important to be as specific as possible. Once you've written the list, read it over to yourself.

Imagine what it feels like to be working in the environment you've designed. It is said, "If you can dream it, you can become it." You may dream big dreams. The world is waiting for you. You are here on purpose.

In the next section, we will continue to explore the reasons for UBS™, stories and more suggested solutions.

What's Driving It: Women's Image Issues
"Be yourself, everyone else is taken." — Anonymous

Women's image issues can start at a very early age. If a girl starts at a young age to think that she has to be a certain way to be pretty or successful, it begins the conditioning of looking at external validation. Advertisements on television or the Internet, national entertainment shows, and reality shows all speak to "this is what pretty looks like, this is what acceptable looks like, and this is what success looks like". Most girls and women don't exactly fit into these categories. Nor, should we want to fit into what popular culture or social conditioning tells us to fit into. We are perfect in our imperfections.

Many products and brands hinge their sales success on a woman or a girl thinking or believing they are "not enough". The media shows girls and women pictures of other girls and women and almost literally states that this is what it looks like to be pretty and successful. The intent of the internet and print ads and television programs may be to sell more products, but some of the messages do sink in.

According to Liaguno, women get manipulated at an early age on image. Women are force fed to be attractive to get the right person or the right situation. Instead of teaching young girls to set a vision for what they want and teach them the ways to do so, our society tells them they are not enough. It puts an inordinate amount of pressure on girls and women. Instead of living authentically and accepting ourselves for who we are, we spend a lot of time and money trying to be someone that we think society, our parents, our spouses/partners, our company or our community wants us to be.

In the workplace, the image issues continue. If a female boss or co-worker with UBS™ considers a female subordinate attractive this can make the boss or co-worker extremely insecure even if she is attractive herself. This is also due to the fact that the female boss' or co-workers with UBS™ cannot internally validate themselves. They tend to judge other people's outsides (appearance, skills, talents, intelligence, personality or behavior) based on their insides (beliefs, strategies, thoughts or emotions).

When female bosses and co-workers with UBS™ see male employees or executives reacting to something positive in another female employee especially if it is her outward appearance, her work, or her demeanor, they tend to resent it. They may not take immediate action to harm or embarrass the female employee, but they will typically, retaliate in some fashion. This is a perceived threat to their survival or success strategies and it cannot be tolerated.

I have observed this behavior in the workplace when a male CEO complimented an attractive female employee regarding her work directly in front of her female boss. Later, the CEO came by the female employee's cubicle to ask another question about the report. In the staff meeting later that week, the female employee was told not to speak directly to the CEO anymore even though the CEO has sought her out on the two occasions mentioned. Two weeks later, she was fired. This may seem like an extreme example, but it happens in small businesses, medium-size companies, and Fortune 50 corporations across the United States and most likely in other countries as well.

Conflict Resolution

Women are taught at an early age how to resolve conflict. Most of their education is learned through observing their parents or other influencing adults in their lives. From an early age, most little girls are taught to resolve things peacefully or through discussions. Many little girls are rewarded or placated by getting what they want after they have a tantrum, raise their voices, pout, or brood. The reinforcement of such behavior leads itself to becoming a habit if not corrected by their early teens. It is a form of conflict resolution by manipulation.

In some cases, when women refer to themselves as "Daddy's girls", they are referring to the fact that they have manipulated their fathers through their behavior as a child to get whatever they want because their fathers didn't want to have conflict with them or see them cry. These same women use these techniques in business with male management and they achieve the same results.

Other little girls become competitive or are encouraged to be competitive with their siblings especially other females as well as their mothers. If this behavior is rewarded, it can also lead to using it as a strategy in their later years. If using manipulation or competitiveness leads to getting what you want at the expense of others, then many young girls are prime candidates to exhibiting UBS™ as adults in the workplace. It's a strategy that has paid off for them their entire lives and has become so familiar that these women are unaware that they are doing it.

In these cases, they typically are not intentionally or consciously aware that they are harming others by it because they are so focused on getting what they want. The act of the manipulation or competitiveness may also be the goal more than the raise, promotion, or getting rid of another female from the position, department, or the company. In other cases, the women are aware they are doing it and they will continue to do it as long as it works for them. They are doing it to achieve any number of things and they are so egotistically driven that it feels like it's anybody's right to do the same if they so choose to do so. The behavior sounds sociopathic. And, it is.

When you think of the term "silent scorn", do you think of a woman or a man? Chances are you may be thinking of a woman. The reason being is that women in general are not taught how to handle conflicts. This is especially true in business.

It must be noted that these assertions are based on my personal experience and the women who were interviewed for the book. Of course, there are women who handle conflict well, those who are trained to do so and those who are natural negotiators. This book is not written about them. They may fall prey to other women who have UBS™ or experience wonderful women in their workplaces. Again, this book is not written about the women who act in a more aware, enlightened way.

Women are traditionally thought of in the feminine as the peacekeepers, mediators, soothers, and supporters. Men are traditionally thought of in the masculine as the aggressors, fighters, rebels, dominators and negotiators. Of course, in most instances, women and men have characteristics that are considered masculine and feminine.

Women with UBS™ are not typically taught how to handle conflict. Therefore, as some of the stories illustrate they become intimidated, jealous, fearful, mean, and destructive. They resolve conflict often by firing their targets. They also may make the person so uncomfortable or fearful that she leaves of her own accord. The strategy becomes more of a chase for more, more, more, and a subconscious belief that there is not enough to go around.

When anyone, including a woman, is driven by the scarcity mentality, then her ability to resolve conflict is skewed. This fear drives most of their decisions. Women suffering from UBS™ will often work extraordinary hours, take extensive travel assignments, skip lunches, skip their family's events (school plays, sporting events, parties) and often, insist on taking on assignments themselves because "their staff is just not capable of handling it."

Conflicts in business often arise out of a company's need to:
- expand or cut back
- limited resources
- competitive pressures

- product or service issues
- lack of customers or satisfied customers
- bad press due to mistakes, misappropriations, poor business practices, social irresponsibility, financial mismanagement, management practices
- too much or not enough exposure or brand perceptions

Baby or No Baby

In the previously mentioned survey on LinkedIn regarding gender preference in bosses, respondents mentioned that female bosses were less likely to be understanding about child care issues than male bosses. This does not stand to reason. Generally speaking, women are still the primary care takers of children and handle the majority of child care needs. Of course, if an employee misses an inordinate amount of work due to issues with a child, or they fundamentally cannot perform their work duties due to their parental role, then it stands to reason that a boss, female or male, needs to address their continued employment with the company. However, there are female bosses with children and those without children who are equally unreasonable about their female workers caring for their children.

The female bosses who have UBS™ may believe that they have made sacrifices in neglecting their children for the good of the company or their own career. They believe their workers should do the same if they want to stay with the company. It speaks to the suppression of feminine characteristics which might be viewed as weak. This is an example of the competitive, ego-driven need to succeed at all costs. The ego is necessary to help us survive. However, when the ego instinct to survive goes awry to survive at all costs then harm will come to anyone who stands in its way.

As in most aspects of UBS™, these women are completely unaware of their behavior and the long-term harm that may impact their female workers and their families. We have all heard people remark that they wish they had spent more time with their kids. I have never heard anyone say that they should spend more time at work and away from their kids.

There are women with UBS™ who do not have children because they didn't choose to or life did not present them with children. They also resent other women who do have children. They do not understand why their female workers need to leave early for appointments, activities, or emergencies for the children. They also have a way of making the women with children feel insecure about their jobs because they are not completely focused on their careers as these women tend to be.

Women's Image Issues
TIRE TRACKS: CHRISTIE

Stacy was hired under the pretense that she was to manage all aspects of a department. Stacy liked Christie, her boss from the beginning. Christie was fun, smart and passionate about the business. She had overcome a personal health challenge and Stacy admired her courage in doing so. Christie had the respect and ear of the members of the executive team especially with Ben, the division executive.

Christie had previously fired Stacy's last three predecessors who were all women. Stacy did not know that at the time she was hired. She also did not know that the company had a major event coming up in less than two months' time. Christie had fired the event manager the same week that Stacy started. Ben was often at the former event planner's desk chatting with her. They would review details about the event and appeared to get along very well. Shortly after that time, the event planner was fired.

Stacy had a daunting task ahead and began to sort through the details of the event plan. She began to realize that the event planner wasn't really an event planner. It was her predecessor who was in charge of the details of the event. The so-called event planner was a sales person that Christie had forced to take the position knowing full well that she would fail. The documentation was a mess. Stacy began to systematically put together all the information into a spreadsheet so she could manage the timeline, budget, sponsorships, hotel, trade show and various other details of the event.

Christie asked Stacy to send her updates of the progress of the event. She initially was okay with Stacy meeting with Ben for the first month. However, Ben started to call Stacy in his office more frequently because he had to approve many of the items being used at the conference as well as determine the sessions and speakers.

Christie would go out of her way to walk by Ben's office as it was not in the same part of the building as her office. She would poke her head in and say, "How are things going with the conference"? When Ben would tell her about a component of the event that was just discussed, Christie said, "Stacy, why haven't you told me about this first?" Stacy said, "We just discussed it now." Christie would mumble under her breath and walk away.

When Stacy returned to her cubicle she would have an email from Christie stating that she wanted the updates to the report immediately and to schedule a meeting to discuss the event. Stacy assumed that Christie was under a lot of pressure and sent her an update along with a meeting request. Christie was never available to meet as Stacy would continue to reschedule based on Christie's calendar. Christie finally agreed to a meeting, Stacy went to meet with her and someone else was sitting in her office. Christie said, "I'll come get you when we're finished." Stacy waited all day while continuing to work on the event. Christie never came by to have a discussion.

Christie sent Stacy an email when it was getting closer to the actual event stating that she would be the one to communicate updates on the event from now on to Ben. Stacy wanted to follow protocol and thought that Christie had her reasons, so she didn't question her directive. Stacy was very pleased that the details of the event were falling into place. The sponsorships were sold out, the trade show was full of exhibitors and a higher amount of customers than usual would be in attendance.

Christie kept asking for details on the event and Stacy would remind her that she sent the reports every Monday and Thursday as requested. Christie said, "why are you not listening to me Stacy, I want the reports twice per week." Stacy thought that maybe something was wrong with her email and asked Christie "can we take a look together to see if you are getting my emails?" Ben would stop by Stacy's cubicle periodically to chat about the event. Christie would walk by and give Stacy dirty looks. Christie would say, "Ben, I'm sorry I must not have been available in my office. Why don't you stop by when you're done with Stacy?"

The first day of the event, Stacy noticed that Christie was not in attendance. Everything appeared to be running smoothly as participants were checking into registration, the keynote sessions and breakout sessions were running on time and without a hitch. The next couple of days began to unravel. Christie began changing the names of the people paired for the golf tournament. She, also, started changing the venues where meals or snacks were served because she said Ben liked it that way.

While watching over one of the breakfasts, Ben came walking down the hallway rather quickly and then began to yell at Stacy. "Don't you know we have always had the continental breakfast served at the gazebo restaurant and not in front of the session rooms? Didn't I make it clear that is the way we did it last year?" Stacy was in shock as Christie did not tell her about that request of Ben's. Stacy had not reviewed the event with Ben directly for two weeks due to Christie's insistence. Several other incidents took place in which Ben was unhappy because his preferences were not occurring at the event. Stacy began to feel sabotaged.

Several vendors and customers came up to Stacy and told her how much they enjoyed the event and that it was one of the best run conferences that they had ever attended. The last day of the event, Christie came up to Stacy in front of Ben and a few other team members and said "why didn't you check with Ben on all these items that were not to his satisfaction? You knew he had final say. What do you have to say for yourself?"

Stacy said "I was following the spreadsheet that you and I discussed." Christie then said," this is not what Ben wanted, you should have checked with him." Stacy was stunned. She excused herself and went into an empty room. Stacy then began to cry and tried to gain her composure. She felt as if Christie had conspired to throw her under the bus. The next Monday, after Stacy had written the event report, Christie called her into a conference room and fired Stacy.

You can continue to read two other Women's Image Issues Tire Tracks or skip to the Solutions section.

Women's Image Issues
TIRE TRACKS: AMY

During Heather's interview for the job at a medical laboratory, Amy was not present. Heather was only supposed to work for Amy for two years and then be transferred to Michael's department. Michael interviewed Heather and they had an immediate rapport. Michael was impressed with Heather's former experience and how she answered all questions in a logical and thorough manner.

Heather was very excited about her new position and her future with the lab. She couldn't wait to get started. On her first day on the job, she had a meeting with Amy. Amy said "I've heard good things about you from Michael. But as a boss, I don't hesitate to fire people." The remark made Heather nervous from the beginning. "I thought she might be joking but she had a serious look on her face when she said it," said Heather.

Heather quickly learned that Amy was the kind of boss where it was her way or the highway. "In every staff meeting, Amy would say that she was open to feedback or input on the topics she had presented," said Heather. She continued, "Anytime that I would speak up about a procedure or a report or any other feedback, Amy would immediately dismiss it or say "no".

"I didn't take it personally at first, but then she did the same thing via email," said Heather. Amy would ask for my input but would never acknowledge what I wrote or let me know if it was viable or not. I would receive accolades from other scientists at the lab, but never an acknowledgement from Amy. I, also, did not know if any of the ideas I presented either verbally or via email were discussed with the executives.

"One day, I received an email from one of the executives, David, asking for a specific list of chemicals for a particular project and my best suggestions for the chemicals. I eagerly and systematically began researching and putting together the list for David. I wanted Amy to know about it so I took the completed list to Amy's office to discuss the request with her," said Heather. Heather was shocked at Amy's reaction. "Why did he contact you and not me for the list? Here give me the list and I'll get back with you with the right information," said Amy. Amy did not get back with Heather and she ignored Heather's emails requesting her input.

David contacted Heather directly again and told her that it had been several days and he needed the list immediately. Heather asked Amy for the list once again stating it was urgent but she did not respond, so Heather sent David the list and copied Amy on the email.

Amy was livid. She replied to both of them and told David that the list was terrible and that she needed more time to revise it. When the revised list was sent to David and Heather the next day, there was only one addition to Heather's original list and it was not a critical item according to Heather.

After several months on the job, Heather experienced a death in her immediate family and her husband was diagnosed with a major illness. Amy appeared to be supportive when Heather needed to take time off. Upon Heather's return to work she was put back into training and made a few mistakes. Heather was upfront about the mistakes and Amy didn't act like the mistakes were a big deal. It was known at the lab that a few of the scientists had made much more critical mistakes and they were not severely reprimanded.

Heather asked to meet with Amy to ask if she would be severely reprimanded or terminated due to the mistakes. Amy said" I know you've been going through a rough time and you don't need to resign over this. Just know that in the event we do let you go, it's nothing personal." The message confused Heather but she thought at the time, Amy was trying to be supportive. Two weeks later, one of Amy's supervisors called Heather into his office and said "you've been put on administrative leave." Heather asked what that meant. He just shrugged and said, "We'll have you speak to my director on Friday."

Walking into the director's office, Heather had a sinking feeling. The director said," I have agreed with the others to let you go. Also, please be advised that Amy has suggested and is documenting that you can never work in a similar lab in this state again." Heather felt completely stung by Amy's remarks and had no idea why Amy hated her so much. Amy told Heather upon her departure, "please know this is not personal, Heather and please feel free to use me as a reference."

Heather was suspicious of Amy offering to be a reference. She hesitantly listed her as a reference as she was applying for a job through a staffing agency. The recruiter called Amy on behalf of a prospective new employer for Heather. The recruiter called Heather and was mortified by what Amy had said. The recruiter proceeded to repeat what Amy said, "I know she's really smart but Heather is a know-it-all and she talks too much. If given the chance, I would not hire her if I were you."

You can continue to read one other Women's Image Issues Tire Tracks or skip to the Solutions section.

Women's Image Issues
TIRE TRACKS: ESTHER

Esther appeared to be the ideal boss. She was very accomplished for being in her early thirties. Esther was promoted to a VP after working her way through the ranks of a technology company. Esther was professional, polished, intelligent, an excellent communicator and attractive. She was married with three children.

Felicia was pleased when she heard that Esther was going to be managing her department. Felicia was in her early twenties and worked hard to be in a supervisory role after only being with the company two years. She was hoping to learn the ropes from Esther because she had admired her professionalism and how articulate she was when she spoke at company meetings. Esther was Felicia's ideal business woman and role model.

The first several months working for Esther seemed to be status quo until she asked the order-entry team to work on weekends. Esther said, "due to the increased sales volume, we will be working weekends, but we won't count that as overtime, so don't put that on your timesheet." Felicia wanted to please Esther and so she did not talk to human resources about having to work on weekends without pay. Esther thought that Felicia must have made sacrifices to have such a high-ranking position with the company so she could make sacrifices too.

One weekend, while she was working, Felicia checked her voicemail and her husband had called with an urgent issue. Felicia called her husband back during the lunch hour. The next Monday, Felicia received an email from Esther stating that she had broken company policy by making a personal phone call at work. Felicia was stunned and angry but she was afraid to speak to anyone about it. She began to feel like Esther was looking for reasons to hold her down. This was perplexing because Esther appeared, at least on the surface, to have her act together.

A few months later, one of Felicia's co-workers, Kathy died suddenly from a brief illness. The funeral was scheduled on a Friday. Felicia went into Esther's office to inform her that she was going to take Friday off in order to go to the funeral and visit with the family afterward. Esther said, "We cannot afford you to take the time off with pay, you will need to put in a vacation day or sick day request in order to take the day off. Plus, keep in mind we are very busy here." Felicia could not believe what she was hearing. The company was doing extremely well. Plus, Kathy (the lady who died) was part of Esther's team and was a wonderful co-worker. She continued that Kathy was a hard worker and she was probably working while she was not feeling well because she was afraid of what Esther would do to her.

"The last straw came for me, when my Dad had a heart attack," said Felicia. She hesitated and continued, I went into Esther's office to tell her about my Dad and to request two weeks off to see my dad on the East coast. This was right around the time when my company was putting the family leave act into policy. Esther said, "You know Felicia this is our busiest time of year, you know we are short staffed (referring to Kathy's death), I just can't let you go at this time."

Felicia had known of another VP named Mike in the company who had made mention of the good work she had done on more than one occasion. She noticed that Mike had a job requisition posted on the company website for a position in his department. Felicia knew she qualified for the position so she applied for the position and put in a request for a transfer.

When Felicia told Esther that she applied for the position in another department, she said "you are too valuable to the department to let you go." However, when she found out that Mike, who had more seniority put a word into the CEO regarding the transfer, Esther called Felicia into her office. Esther stated in a very harsh tone, "I never really thought you fit well with the team, I am going to transfer you to Mike's department.

Felicia was elated on the inside and told Esther, "As you wish." When Felicia met with Mike for the first time, she told him that her father had a heart attack last week and she didn't know what to do about it. Felicia continued, "Esther said it's our busiest season and…" Before she could finish her sentence, Mike interrupted her and said, "you need to leave this afternoon- go on get out of here. Please call me once you assess the situation and let me know how much time you need. Your family is important."

Felicia said, "I always felt that Esther was trying to hold me down and I have no idea why. She had so much going for her. I used to look up to her until I knew what she was like. I went to work for Mike and never looked back. It's a shame too because I thought I could learn from Esther. I did learn from her. I learned about the type of manager that I never want to be."

Women's Image Issues
SUGGESTED SOLUTIONS

"When you are inspired by some great purpose, some extraordinary project, all your thoughts break their bonds; your mind transcends limitations your consciousness expands in every direction, and you find yourself in a new, great and wonderful world. Dormant forces, faculties and talents come alive, and you discover yourself to be a greater person by far than you ever dreamed yourself to be." – Pantanjali

Be Driven by Passion and Purpose

Take the information from your visioning and highlight the words, phrases and activities that keep showing up. Now, write them or type them out on a separate file or piece of paper. Make a note of the activities that you love to do. How do they align with various jobs or careers?

Next to each line item on the page, think of all the different types of jobs or careers that involve what you have written. Get creative and try to think as expansively as you can. Take your time. There are two ways to approach the list. You can complete all of it in one sitting or you can take each line item and focus on them individually. If you take the individual route, it is suggested to prioritize the list first to those activities you enjoy the most in descending order or from the most to the least.

Once you have determined the professions that are most involved with the type of activities that you enjoy doing and that make your heart happy, then look at how you can explore them further. For example, you may wish to go to school or take a certification course on the subject. You may also wish to call people who are working in that field and ask them if you can take them to coffee for an informational interview. There are also trade associations that host monthly meetings and it would be a good idea to go to one of those meetings to make contacts. Linkedin.com provides a wealth of groups who specialize in many different industries and occupations. You may wish to join some of these groups or find out who is the group administrator and contact them about your interest.

It may be worth your while to contact a life coach and or career coach to see if she or he can assist you with the information you gathered about yourself. It's always good to have mentors and accountability partners to help you set your goals and to keep you on track. Most successful women in business and life have several mentors, coaches, and accountability partners. If more women had these types of advocates, then it is highly likely that UBS™ would disappear altogether.

Why This Test Drive Works

"The reason why visioning and passion searches work is because they are internally validating," says Liaguno. The information is based on what makes you happy and what gives you a sense of purpose and fulfillment. It's not a cookie cutter approach. It's not dictated by society or by the scarcity mentality or by women's image issues. It reaches into your dreams and aspirations. It is truly an authentic response to what you want to express through your occupation or path.

"You are loved just for being who you are, just for existing. You don't have to do anything to earn it. Your shortcomings, your lack of self-esteem, physical perfection or social and economic success – none of that matters. No one can take this love away from you, and it will always be here." – Ram Dass

The number one reason that most women are not as successful in business is due to their own thoughts, feelings and actions about themselves. Secondarily, we do not have enough women who are being mentors to other women. This situation is changing and I would like all of us to be a part of that change. Our allowing of defeatist thinking in any aspect of life and especially in business will most likely hinder or negate bringing about any positive change or results for ourselves or others.

We as women often tell ourselves that we are not enough – not talented enough, not smart enough, not capable enough, too old, too young, under qualified, over qualified, too thin, too fat – the list goes on and on. It truly is an authentic response to what you want to express through your occupation or path. The following excerpt is a perfect example of how we can transform our thoughts, feelings, and actions to become what we were intended to be.

The Auto Flog Switch™ and Affirmations

At an early age, I started to believe that I was not good enough. I personally installed what I call the "Auto Flog Switch™" and I jammed it to on quite frequently. When I made a mistake or a perceived mistake, I would be harder on myself than anyone else could be on me. Negative self-talk was a frequent mantra. When I was in my early 20's, I realized that the Auto Flog switch was not serving me at all.

Auto-Flog Switch™

A self-installed, figurative switch that automatically connects a woman to negative and defeatist thinking and feeling to keep her feeling poorly about herself. It's painful and not in a good way.

Recently while I was meeting with a coaching client, I mentioned the Auto Flog Switch™. She laughed, "She said I never named it as such but that is exactly what I do when I make a mistake." When I mentioned this tendency or the switch as I named it to the women whom I interviewed, literally every one of them said they start the negative self-talk automatically.

As mentioned under the solutions section of the Scarcity Mentality, affirmations broke my Auto Flog Switch. Instead of my saying something negative about myself, I would switch it to an affirmation.

Another suggested solution, when I would catch myself saying, "You're not good enough." I would say, mostly silently, "thanks for sharing, I am good enough."

Letting go of judgment by changing your breathing pattern is also recommended. As discussed previously.

The Wheels of the Bus go round and round – Women's cycling

As most women are aware, we have hormonal changes in our bodies. However, we often are not aware how these hormones affect how we act, think and feel at work.

Before and during menstrual cycles, we might become irritable, angry, anxious, sad, frustrated, disappointed, and a whole host of emotions and feelings. Many women have difficulty concentrating and thinking clearly before, during, or after their periods.

It's important for women during their child bearing years to know their cycles, when they're ovulating and when you're menstruating that you may be slightly or entirely run by your hormones. Having this awareness will allow you to know that you may be oversensitive to the actions and words of others. You might tend to react to others instead of responding. You might bite their heads off or you might start crying in front of them. Pregnancy may also bring about hormonal changes that will affect your mood, feelings, and cognitive abilities.

If you are no longer having consistent periods, are not pregnant, and you are experience peri-menopause or starting menopause itself, you may also experience hormonal changes that mess with your moods, feelings, and thinking. This cessation of your menstrual cycle can cause hot flashes, night sweats, day sweats, mood swings, and other symptoms. Again, awareness is the key.

To quote the country singer, Tammy Wynette, "sometimes it's hard to be a woman." While we get to experience the joys of carrying a baby, we also get to experience all that comes with it. That is why it is so important to be aware of your time in your cycle of life as well as the women around you. Plus, scientific studies have proven that women who work together over an extended period of time tend to cycle together.

The suggested solution is to think about where you are on your cycle when you find you being overly sensitive, sad, angry or irritable on the job. Ask yourself if your mood is in response to or being affected by your hormones. Make sure you are taking extra care of yourself and not taking it out unnecessarily on yourself or your co-workers. Also, make sure you are getting the rest and possibly medication or natural supplements you need.

H. A. L. T. – Hungry, Angry, Lonely, Tired
A dear friend of mine in a recovery program said to me, "you must be experiencing HALT." When I inquired further, she told me that I had been traveling, not eating regularly, and I wasn't getting enough sleep. She knew that I was working at a very large company event that I had to manage and I was neglecting to take care of myself.
How many of us juggle - kids, extracurricular activities, hobbies, work, significant

others, spouses, friends, pets, work? The lists can go on infinitum. This can completely affect our mood or our attitudes toward us, our co-workers and lives. Juggling can make a woman hungry, angry, lonely, and tired.

Minutiae which would normally escape our view become a BIG deal. We get tripped up about it. We lose our cool. We start to take it out on those around us who don't deserve it. We might even begin to beat ourselves up about it and become irritable and depressed.

By definition, the word halt is to stop, cease, or pause. Basically, if you find yourself feeling really upset over something instead of taking it out on a coworker, subordinate, boss or management, stop and ask yourself, am I hungry, angry, lonely, or tired?

During the movie, Best in Show when Christopher Guest's character was leaving with his hound dog to go to the dog show his friend yells out, "if you're hungry eat, if you're tired rest." It may sound simple, but it's sage advice. The more awareness you have about your mind, body, and emotions, the more aware you will be of your moods and how to change them.

What's Driving It - Masculine versus Feminine Acceptance

"A woman should keep her separateness, should save all her feminine qualities and purify them. In this way she is going, according to her nature, towards enlightenment. Of course once you are enlightened, you have gone beyond the discrimination of sexes. Beyond enlightenment, you are simply human beings. But before that.... Be proud of your qualities. Increase them, refine them. I would like the whole world to be full of feminine qualities. - Osho

In business and society, the qualities of masculinity have been highly valued. It is pervasive in sports, entertainment, business, politics, and culture overall. These characteristics generally attributed to men or boys are competitiveness, aggression, vigor, boldness, forcefulness, strength, courage, and assertion. While the characteristics generally attributed to women or girls are gentleness, kindness, weakness, modesty, and supportiveness.

Most men and women have varying combinations of both masculine and feminine characteristics which are not gender specific. Living authentically means embracing the characteristics that are inherent within each of us, individually, and not trying to live as we are socially conditioned to believe we should be. However, the predominant nature of Western society conditions women to use masculine qualities to survive and succeed. Men act like men. Women act like men to survive and succeed. It's become more of a life strategy. This strategy does not allow women to be their authentic selves. It undermines, confuses, conflicts, and makes it difficult for many women to get past their social conditioning.

There are women who use their feminine qualities as a strategy in business to flirt, cajole, manipulate, or sleep their way to the top. They, too, are most likely not being authentic to themselves but use this as a life strategy to succeed or survive. Most of us have heard of the "casting couch" or have watched one or more of our female bosses or co-workers shamelessly flirt with an executive or all of sudden disappear together at a company function.

The other underlying dynamic which is becoming more and more pervasive, and not just in the United States, is attaching self-worth or our authentic selves to what we do for a living or what we have. Our occupations, hobbies, social circles as well as our material wealth, toys, vacations, properties, stocks, bonds are externalized sources. Instead of living true to our authentic selves and acting as human beings or an internalized source, we judge and are judged by what we do and have – "human doings" or "human havings".

This makes it extremely difficult for women who feel a strong desire to have and do what others do or have. These same women may also believe that in order to be judged as a success, they have to have or do what others have or do. These professions or material things are used to puff up their egos like an overinflated balloon. Eventually, the balloons deflate because the "doing and having" is not internally validating. In other words, it's not done from a place of authenticity. The doing or having is an external approval strategy or a survival strategy.

There are those women who, also, are continually in the elusive pursuit of more or better. They are so focused on achieving a title, promotion, project, award, material wealth that they will step over or annihilate anyone who gets in their way, especially the nearest female on their path. Again this book does not represent all women in business; however, it does bring to the spotlight the women who throw other women under the bus in their elusive pursuit for more or better.

Momma versus Me

If you look at the history of many women who exhibit UBS™ in the workplace, you might want to first start with their mothers. Yes, believe it or not this is learned behavior. In a quest to receive love or attention, these mothers begin to compete with their daughters. They don't know how to be internally validating so they continue to seek external validation even if it's at the expense of their daughters' self-esteem.

As the daughters become teenagers, they may begin to get compliments or attention from other people and their mothers take notice. These mothers, consciously or unconsciously are setting their daughters up to have UBS™.

These women are insecure. Instead of being proud of their daughters, they see them as competition. They will go to various lengths including plastic surgery, flirting with objects of their daughter's affection such as, a boyfriend, or simply saying or doing things that negatively impact their daughter's self-esteem. The words or actions may be used as a manipulative method of trying to protect the daughter against disappointment. The truth is, it's an expression of the mother's own disappointment with herself.

It is very difficult for women with UBS™ who have had a competitive mother to see this behavior in themselves. The reasons for the difficulty are complex. A mother is an authority figure and a child believes that how the authority figure acts is "the way to act". These women are being conditioned to behave in that manner. It may also set up a life-long quest to seek the mother's approval which may only come if the daughter succeeds in business at all costs. This means taking down or throwing other women under the bus.

Once a Brat Always a Brat
One day last summer, I accepted an invitation for coffee to meet with a woman who was a friend of a friend. She said that she had alienated everyone in her life and she wanted to reach out and make more female friends. As I am a proponent of women and I found her alienation story interesting, I accepted her invitation. Plus, she sounded like an UBSer™. And, I wanted to learn from her perspective.
Helene (not her real name) turned out to be a lovely person. She was energetic, intelligent, accomplished, and friendly. She seemed to take an interest when she asked me about myself.

We became fast friends and continued to meet for coffee on a regular basis. Over the course of our discussions, she inquired about the book I was writing. I told her the topic and when I began to explain the traits of an UBSer™, she blurted out, "I am that woman." Helene continued to say that she would throw other women under the bus or compete so strongly against them that she would eventually win out. I was perplexed by this and told her that she comes across as a truly wonderful person who makes friends easily and is certainly capable and confident.

She continued to tell me that she doesn't have any girlfriends, would prefer to work with guys, sees other women as competition, and is jealous of their successes. She said that this has made her truly lonely, overly dependent on her boyfriend and really wanting to change how she is to other people and especially women.

I asked her, "what do you think are the reasons that you act that way?" She remarked "because I'm a spoiled brat. I have always been a spoiled brat. You see, I'm an only child and I'm used to getting my way. If I don't get what I want, I act out and become upset. Either that or I turn on the charm."

I was shocked by her candor. She said that she was acting this way in business as well. "I've been in sales for a long time. If one of the other women is selling more than me or appears to be getting along with a customer better than I do, I get jealous. I find myself speaking ill of her to management or other employees or I try to get her territory pulled from her and given to me," said Helene.
"What made you want to change the behavior?" I inquired. Helene said, "I noticed another woman in the office acting the same way and thought what an ugly person." She continued and "I, then, realized, I'm pretty ugly myself."

"It no longer felt right to continue acting like I did. I realized that deep down, I'm really insecure and I used my charm or my bullying to get what I wanted like I did as a child," said Helene. "It gave me a pain in the pit of my stomach."

"Once I had the awareness of what I was doing and that I was doing it so unconsciously and especially to women, I had to look at what I was so angry about," said Helene. "I realized that it was my insecurity all along and that not everybody was like my parents and responds to emotional blackmail", she said. "I wanted what I wanted when I wanted it," said Helene. "That sounds like a brat doesn't it?" she asked. "Yes and an UBSer™," said I. We both laughed.

Masculinity is Overvalued

In Western society as in business in general, masculine characteristics are overvalued. In order to succeed, men and women have had to exhibit what was considered masculine characteristics, such as, being bold and aggressive. Even some of the women's movements have been masculine in their approach to infiltrate and overcome the organizations that were once predominantly patronized by and comprised of men. Feminine characteristics such as being nurturing and gentle were embraced more on the non-profit side of business as they catered to human services and social programs. They were not highly regarded as qualities sought for an executive in general business.

There were, also, examples of women exhibiting feminine characteristics such as becoming overtly charming and flirty to get what they want as well. This can be a form of UBS™ when these women will use these characteristics even if they morally or ethically cross the line of others. As masculine characteristics are more highly regarded in business, it lends itself to an understanding why so many women utilize these characteristics as part of their overall survival and success strategies.

This strategy starts in childhood as we don't know who we are and we are trying to fit into the world. We don't allow ourselves to be authentic. As mentioned in a previous section, most of us are a combination of masculine and feminine characteristics that are not dependent on our gender.

The main reason that women get UBS™ is that they are not conscious or aware enough. They don't have a real vision of who they are. They are caught up in "doing and having" and identifying with the doing and having. They can't do and have enough. All the doing and having is to get to who they want to be. Basically, it's completely looking outside of themselves for the answers.

Instead of creating their own vision for themselves, women become part of the herd. They are forcing themselves to be a version of pretty, president, a cheerleader or married. Nothing is wrong with any of these things if they are authentic to themselves and their vision. The fear of being ostracized, unaccepted or unsuccessful by someone else's standards is what's driving Under the Bus Syndrome™.

Masculine vs. Feminine Acceptance
TIRE TRACKS: RACHEL

Jennifer was working as a human resources (HR) generalist for about four years at a thriving non-profit on the West coast. She and her co-worker and boss, Rene, were searching for a new CEO for the non-profit for months. Rene was very excited when she finally found the ideal candidate for the position. The candidate, Rachel, was dynamic, bright and had an HR background. She lived on the East coast and said that she had no problem in being in the West coast office several weeks out of the month.

Rachel was hired and initially she was very well liked and respected. Rachel came to the West coast office to meet individually with the staff. According to Jennifer, Rachel was very intelligent and charismatic. "I remember that she took the time to get to know a little bit about me," said Jennifer. "She was a breath of fresh air as the former CEO was very cold and distant with the staff," Jennifer continued. "Rachel told us that our jobs were secure and that the headquarters were going to stay on the West Coast. I really liked her. She was really adorable and charming," said Jennifer.

Within one month of employment, Rachel made an announcement that the Company would be headquartered on the East coast in title only. She told the staff via a series of announcements that nothing would change especially in the HR function. Jennifer was very happy at this point because one of Rachel's emails said that our HR team is phenomenal. "She told us not to worry again because our jobs are secure," said Jennifer.

Rachel was hired in October and by January at least five people were being laid off per month at the company. Jennifer said," Sadly, she made us do all the layoffs. " "She was never at the West coast office. She had a huge corner office and she never came in," Jennifer continued.

The company started to lose money but it did not stop Rachel from having expensive fundraising events where she would be hiring or hobnobbing with celebrities. She would create these huge events with celebrities where she would have the media present to interview her and take pictures with well-known celebrities on the East coast. She was very much into self-promotion. Jennifer remarked that Rachel was so self-absorbed that she had the audacity to call the corporate communication manager to write a press release about her on Christmas Eve. The press release was not urgent and had little to do with the Company and everything to do about Rachel. Jennifer stated that meanwhile she was continuing to lay people off and everyone in the company was forced to drastically cut expenses except Rachel.

In August of the same year, after telling the HR team that their jobs were secure, Rachel had the Chief Operating Officer (COO) of the Company deliver the bad news to Jennifer. "The team was called into the COO's office and told that our jobs would be eliminated and the last day would be December 1st," said Jennifer. Jennifer was told that all of her functions would be eliminated and she was to focus on recruiting the replacement people for the new East coast headquarters. The West coast office would be closing.

"This was completely opposite of what Rachel said when she was hired," said Jennifer. "It was extremely difficult to recruit for positions when my job was being eliminated. I was forced to omit information to the candidates I was recruiting knowing full well that I was losing my job three weeks before Christmas," Jennifer continued. "She threw all of us under the bus to get what she wanted in the first place," said Jennifer.

One year later, Jennifer was baffled by Rachel. She received a Christmas card from Rachel asking for a donation for the struggling non- profit which was located on the East coast.

Masculine vs. Feminine Acceptance
TIRE TRACKS: MARY JANE

Fiona quickly packed her belongings into several boxes. She was excited to move to another department within a multibillion-dollar technology company. She had worked for the CEO previously at another thriving technology company and had absolute respect and admiration for his business acumen, management style and his treatment of his employees. The company was growing and she knew that if she worked hard enough, her career would advance as the company continued to grow.

She worked for Tim for a couple of years. He had a reputation for being a bully and she experienced it first-hand too many times. When she was asked by Mary Jane at the behest of the CEO to join Mary Jane's team, she jumped at the chance.

Although she had not worked with Mary Jane previously, she heard great things about her from some of the guys on the management team. She did not think to ask any of the female executives about her. Mary Jane was very professional, reserved and polished in the way she presented herself. Fiona thought, "Mary Jane is well educated, professional and has business savvy. I look forward to working with her. I know I can learn a lot from her. Maybe, she can become my mentor."

"In the beginning, I learned a tremendous amount from Mary Jane," said Fiona. "She did treat me as if I was her protégé. She knew that I had worked for the CEO prior to my joining the company and initially was pleased that I had a good relationship with him," said Fiona.

She continued, "Mary Jane was never exactly what you would call warm to me, but she taught me many and varied aspects of the business which I appreciated. I had a knack for building relationships with our technology vendors. Mary Jane never was able to build good rapport with them because she was so reserved and often suspicious of them. I didn't think our different styles would be a problem."

"I began to notice how Mary Jane would look me up and down when we had meetings. It was as if she was judging or disapproving of me. I don't mean to sound arrogant, but I'm an attractive woman and I always would dress in a professional manner but definitely feminine. Mary Jane would dress professional but very corporate, business-like and in suits that were borderline masculine. After about six months, things began to unravel," said Fiona.

Fiona stated "Mary Jane became really critical of my work. She used to encourage me to come up with new ideas and treated me as if I had a truly innovative mind. "She would literally shoot down every idea I came up with," said Fiona. She continued, Mary Jane would find a way to shoot down my ideas publicly. This continued for some time then one day she set me up.

The company was planning to implement a very lucrative, national program for its clients. There was a tremendous opportunity to get vendor sponsorship. While we were being briefed by the CEO on the opportunity, I was coming up with ideas on how to approach my vendor partners and show them the value and benefits of their participation.

After the briefing, Mary Jane called me into a meeting with her to discuss our strategies and tactics for the program. "I spoke with her for about an hour and told her of the all the ideas I had in getting the vendor sponsorship, which vendors would most likely participate, and at what levels," said Fiona. She continued "I ran similar strategies and tactics with my vendor partners previously and was extremely successful with them. The vendors were always pleased with me too. We had a trust factor in how we did business together and I valued their partnership."

"Mary Jane insisted I take the strategies and tactics in a different direction than I explained. She basically asked me to lie to the vendor managers whom I had built relationships on mutual trust," said Fiona.

"It blew up. When the vendors complained and they did complain rather loud, Mary Jane said that it was completely my idea," said Fiona. Sadly, a few of the vendors asked her if I could be taken off their accounts, she continued.

Fiona stated that all Mary Jane's decisions were based on making her look good and others look bad. When I stepped back and observed her, I began to notice that her ruthlessness was directed primarily at women. "She was a political animal. She couldn't fire me because she knew I had allies in management but that didn't stop her from completely stalling my career and making me look bad to my vendors, said Fiona.

Fiona continued, I had a good working relationship with many of the males in the company whom I worked with previously at the other company and she resented it. I was an "attractive risk factor" so she tried to position me as an airhead. I used feminine qualities in business and she did not. She treated me as if being feminine and professional was unacceptable. She acted cold and dressed more like a man.

"It was awful. I thought I was stuck and would not get promoted anywhere in the company unless she gets promoted and hopefully, away from running the department," said Fiona. "Luckily, the CEO started a new division and asked me if I was interested in going to work there. I know Mary Jane wanted to stop the move but the CEO allowed it," said Fiona.

"Mary Jane rarely spoke to me after that. On the off chance she did, it was rather curt and cold," said Fiona. Fiona continued that I never told management about her because I didn't want to do to her what she did to me.

"My next boss was a female. I went into working for her with trepidation but she turned out to be terrific," said Fiona.

You can continue to read one other Women's Image Issues Tire Tracks or skip to the Solutions section.

Masculine vs. Feminine Acceptance
TIRE TRACKS: JANET

As the Executive Director of a non-profit agency I worked with Janet for over nine years. The first several years we worked well together. She was a terrific employee. Her work was impeccable; she communicated well and had a great rapport with our clients and the board of directors. "I felt that no matter what would come our way, Janet had my back," said Thea.

I didn't socialize frequently with Janet outside of the office. On the occasions we did get together, she was very warm and friendly to my husband and my elderly mother. She and her husband took a particular interest in helping my mother with miscellaneous projects around her house and this really touched my heart. I was, also, very supportive of her, her husband, and daughter.

Most of the projects at the agency were handled directly by me or by Janet and her staff. For the most part, everything ran very smoothly. One day at the agency we were thrilled because we were awarded a state-run project which would allow us to expand.

There were two segments to the project. One segment was to be run by Janet who referred children and their families to healthcare services. The other segment would be run by a new employee who would then take the referrals from Janet and provide case management for their healthcare services through a designated hospital system.

I hired Sue for the position to provide case management along with a team to support her efforts. "Initially, for about four months, Sue and Janet got along well," said Thea. She continued, Janet was referring clients and Sue was getting them in the system and providing case management to ensure they received quality healthcare services according to their individual needs.

"I can't put my finger on any particular incident or aspect of Sue's personality, but Janet began to systematically try to ruin her reputation and taint the program overall," said Thea. "Her disdain for Sue began to turn Janet into a monster. It was a real shock too because I thought so highly of Janet and her work. It all began with Janet lying to me," said Thea.

"We were about six months into the program when Sue told me that she was hardly getting any referrals to the case managers assigned to the program. I told her that I would look into it," said Thea.

"I called Janet into my office to inquire how she was doing and how the program was going. I've always been a hands-off manager because I trust my employees. I only get involved when we need extra support, my employees ask me to do so or if the board suggests it," Thea continued.

Thea stated that Janet was insistent that she was referring the enrolled children into case management and was curious as to why they were not meeting with the case managers. "She assured me that the program was running smoothly. I asked her about her working relationship with Sue and she said that everything was going well. I had no reason to distrust what she was saying as her reports explicitly showed a large amount of children enrolling in the program," said Thea.

"Janet began contacting people at the state level and was bad mouthing the case management portion of the project. She had reportedly told them that the program was unsuccessful and that Sue was completely incompetent. She also started telling the community partners who supported the program the same type of nonsense," said Thea.

"Several of the community partners told me that Janet was providing misinformation and gossiping about Sue and the program," said Thea. "I didn't want to believe it; I thought the world of Janet professionally and personally. In the past, she was very appropriate, professional and acted like a team player. She would back the agency, its programs and me. Unfortunately, this is not the saddest part of the story," she continued.

"I called Janet into my office and told her I was aware of the fact she was not referring people to Sue and the case management team. I, also, told her that I was aware of her speaking ill of the program and Sue and that it had to stop immediately," said Thea. "She took it as a call to war and I became an object of her anger and reproach," she said.

Thea said that Janet contacted people at the state level who were in charge of the program and again spoke ill of Sue and the case management aspect of the program. "I knew this for a fact because I received a call that very same afternoon from a state-level contact telling me that Janet was bad-mouthing the program and Sue. I was reprimanded and told in no uncertain terms that 'I needed to fix it', said Thea.

The next morning I met with Janet. "I'm a direct communicator, so I told Janet that I received a call from a state official about her bad mouthing the program and our staff. She flat out denied it and said it was taken entirely out of context," said Thea.

"Janet's cut-throat behavior did not stop there. She met with the hospital staff including one of our board members as part of her program. She continued to bad mouth the program and Sue. She said that it was not as successful as the agency hoped. However, she completely out stepped her bounds by stating the overall program needed only one more staff member for the next fiscal year because our clients were not utilizing the case management portion of it," said Thea.

"When I had the official meeting with the hospital staff including the board member, I presented the overall program, its successes, its areas of improvement and the required staff for the following year. In my presentation, I was requesting funding for three additional positions as they were in exact proportion to the growth of the program," said Thea.

"The hospital staff was absolutely livid with me. I don't recall being in a more hostile meeting in my life. One staff member screamed at me and said we were told that you only needed one additional staff member. He continued that we did not budget for it and you have some nerve coming in here asking for more when we were assured that you needed only one," said Thea.

"Sue looked at me as if she was in shock. Janet just sat there and said nothing. She wouldn't even look at me," said Thea.

"The next day, the board member called me and said I think Janet intentionally set you up. She is, also, not doing you any favors with the state, hospital staff or me," said Thea.

She sadly continued that when she asked Janet again about meeting secretly with the hospital staff or bad mouthing the program and now the agency, she flat out denied it. "My credibility was shot, everyone thought that the program was poor, I was a bad manager and that the agency overall was unprofessional and disorganized," said Thea.

"I since moved on to run another non-profit agency. The last I heard about Janet is that she was trying to get her daughter in a position with a state agency that would oversee a program that Sue was working on. To this day, I have no idea what she has against Sue or why she had to take me down because I couldn't condone her behavior. It's so strange to me because Janet was so bright, talented, and competent at her job," said Thea.

Masculine vs. Feminine Acceptance
SUGGESTED SOLUTIONS

"Your health is your responsibility." – Jillian Michaels

Go Forward for the long run
There have been and will continue to be a million and one books, blogs, programs, and videos on the subject of physical exercise. Yes, it is beneficial to us in a myriad of ways – controls weight, builds endurance and stamina, releases positive endorphins in our brains, stimulates muscle groups, helps with blood flow, increases oxygen to the brain, relieves stress, and uplifts overall mood.

Yes, that sounds great, but it takes effort. How can I, a victim of an UBSer™ or me, the UBSer™ find time in my schedule to exercise? The answer is in the question.

Being run by the scarcity mentality of more, more, more or never enough, we women run ourselves' ragged. We work, take care of the kids, partners and pets, manage the household, manage the kids extracurricular activities, run business meetings, write reports, develop new business, meet with customers, staff, and vendors. We have become human doings. We are not human beings because we don't have the awareness to stop and take the time to just be.

I understand that most of the aforementioned activities are obligations, so why not be obliged to schedule exercise as well.

 In order to find time, we have to make ourselves a priority. Exercise does not have to mean that you are going to start to compete in Iron Woman competitions or have to get down to zero percent body fat to make it worthwhile.

Exercise will be most effective, if it is something that you enjoy doing and you can schedule it for at least 30 minutes per session, several times per week. It may be helpful to get a workout buddy, someone who will go with you to the gym, on a walk, or whom will join a recreational sports team with you. The point is to get moving – for fun.

Realistically, as with many aspects of life, you might be into a particular sport or activity for years and then stop it completely. It's important to continue to find ways of exercising that you enjoy as your interests expand and change. Plus, while you're exercising, it's a great time to say your positive affirmations or make the experience a meditative one.

Mentoring

"It is our light not our darkness that most frightens us. Our deepest fear is not that we are inadequate. Our deepest fear is that we are powerful beyond measure. It is our light not our darkness that most frightens us. We ask ourselves, who am I to be brilliant, gorgeous, talented and fabulous? Actually, who are you not to be? You are a child of God. Your playing small does not serve the world. There's nothing enlightened about shrinking so that other people won't feel insecure around you. We were born to make manifest the glory of God that is within us. It's not just in some of us; it's in everyone. As we let our own light shine, we unconsciously give other people permission to do the same. As we are liberated from our own fear, our presence automatically liberates others." -Marianne Williamson

Once you have become more internally validating or if you have a clear vision of your career, then it may be a good time to look at becoming a mentor. As it's said, you can't transmit something you haven't got. If you are acting under UBS™, you probably will not want to mentor. However, it's probably safe for me to assume that most of you who are reading this have plenty of knowledge, experience and skills that you can share. Plus, you have overcome or are healing from UBS™ or your experience with your UBSer™.

There is another saying; it states that you can only keep something by giving it away. Below are suggestions for mentoring:

Your Company
No matter how long you've been in business or at your company, you have talents and skills that you can lend to your female coworkers, boss or subordinates. Mentoring comes in many forms besides one-on-one coaching or connecting. If you work for a very large corporation, you may wish to check with your human resources department to see if they have any affiliations or mentoring programs for the women in your company.

No matter the size of your company or business, at the very least, you can make a commitment to yourself that you will help or guide other women in your company. You can be of assistance to everyone but especially other women whenever it is possible within the context of your particular role with the company. It is not surprising what a little guidance or a few words of encouragement can do to help another person boost their confidence or productivity.

Your Connections
Whether you keep in contact with your women business associates through email, Facebook, Linkedin, your website, your newsletter, blog, or phone calls, you have a list of women who can form a community for mentoring, support, encouragement, and accountability. You can contact them to see how you might be able to help them or set up a forum by which you can communicate, collaborate, and help mentor each other. More than likely, you have a diverse group of women who have a lot to offer each other. They didn't know this before, but you can be the catalyst for this connection.

Your contacts may also be able to connect you and the others to women's organizations in which they belong. This is one of the best ways to get on the bus together instead of using it as a weapon. It's empowering. It allows you to expand your ideas, talents and sharing well beyond anything you could do on your own. Plus, it benefits all the women involved.

Your Community
No matter how large or small the population of the city where you live, you can either find or create a woman's business network. In the early 1800's women started the suffrage movement which allowed women to vote in national elections in the United States. We were not allowed a voice in politics until that time. Since that time, we have seen the likes of Margaret Thatcher, Bhutros Bhutros Galli, Indira Ghandi, Condalisa Rice, Hillary Clinton and others hold some of the highest political offices in their respective countries around the world. If you don't know who any of these women are, I would suggest you research them. Whether you agree with their politics or not, they have paved a path of greatness for us.

I am not suggesting that you go into politics. However, I am suggesting that any positive ideas have to start somewhere, so why not with you? If you don't have a women's business organization in your community, perhaps you can contact a national organization and ask how to start a branch or group in your town. You might also want to start a group or meeting and invite business women to speak on a variety of topics.

If you belong to a particular industry and want to be an advocate of women in that industry, check to see if any associations exist. If not, you might look at forming an association to do so.

Women Empowered in the World

Women who are empowered in the world are a force to be celebrated. We have the opportunity and energy to create a work environment that fosters growth, peace, and fulfillment. When we, as empowered women who are aware of our mind, muscles, moods and our ability to mentor come together, we will be able to change the world one workplace at a time.

Chapter Four
TELL TALE SIGNS YOU'RE GOING UNDER THE BUS

During the interview process of this book, many of the women who were victims of other women with UBS™ spoke of signs these women exhibited. Realistically, we have all displayed a few of these signs during our working lives. The difference between an UBSer™ and your average gal on the job is that a high number of these signs are observed and on a frequent basis. These actions emerge as part of a life strategy or an underlying dynamic of the UBSer™.

Here are the tell-tale signs which were mentioned repeatedly in my experience, interviews and research.
- Gossiping about other women
- Speaking ill of other women during the interview process
- Withholding critical information
- Taking credit for other's work
- Blaming others for errors, mistakes and screw ups which were hers (gal with UBS™ or UBSer's™) responsibility
- Acting jealous, threatened, hostile or insecure
- Not allowing the other female(s) to communicate with management, other departments
- Telling the female employee that everything is fine regarding her performance and complaining about her performance to others
- Acting unduly angry or frustrated with reasonable requests for family or child care
- Saying cruel or demeaning remarks to a female employee when no one is

around to witness it
- Being overly competitive or specifically/deliberately denying or withholding information resources, promotions, transfers which would make the female employee successful
- Overly flirting, manipulating or showing favoritism to male counterparts or management

The difficulty that many women face in the workplace is that they deny or ignore these signs until it is too late. Either the person with UBS™ has thrown them under the bus or they are so disillusioned with their employment that they quit of their own accord.

Often these signs are ignored or denied because they might be done on a lesser or more subtle degree. Many times the women with UBS™ are very charismatic and it's so hard to believe they can be so ruthless when they "once" were so kind or genuine. As in most dysfunctional relationships, it's difficult to imagine that anyone who has some great qualities can be so harmful. Many of the women remarked about one instance of kindness or a period of time when the boss or co-worker seemed so professional, reasonable or pleasant which would initially make all the subsequent ill behaviors seem unbelievable. To a greater or lesser degree, women with UBS™ can be correlated to an abusive partner. They can be very charming and sweet, but systematically begin to assert behavior that is quite unsavory, unkind, and threatening.

While this is a difficult or unheard of classification of a syndrome in psychological or human resources annals, it is a syndrome just the same. Knowing the signs of UBS™ can assist in awareness and identification of it. However, it is not yet accepted in technical or other terms in human resources training manuals or in employment law. Nor should UBS™ be used for more litigation or conflict purposes.

Chapter Five
A STRONG WOMAN VERSUS AN UBSer™

Almost every woman whom I interviewed said there is distinct difference between a strong woman and an UBSer™.

There are general characteristics that could describe a strong woman and an UBSer™ alike. They may be confident, skilled, talented, professional, intelligent, astute and qualified. Other potentially shared characteristics are assertiveness, charismatic, provocative, eloquent, and motivated. In both instances, these two types are typically women who stand up for their beliefs and they are not afraid to confront or discuss issues that others tend to ignore or shy away from. Of course, not every strong woman or UBSer™ embodies all of the aforementioned traits.

The fundamental difference is that strong women don't use these traits as a strategy for their own gain, to hide their insecurities or to tow the company line even if it's detrimental to the company. Strong women often make it a personal goal to uplift those around them. They will try to encourage, enlighten, and promote others knowing that they can achieve their goals if they help others do the same.

"My former boss, Ellen always worked collaboratively with us to achieve our department goals. She consistently looked at ways to bring us the education, tools, and resources to make us each successful. She spoke about empowerment and she lived it through how she treated us," said Isabelle.

UBSers™ have used certain life strategies for such a long time that they are making those around them suffer. "The biggest problem I had with my boss is that at times she was compassionate towards me but she would quickly turn on me if she thought it made her look bad or when she didn't want to stand up for me," said Theresa.

It's not that UBSers™ are constantly acting out in negative, demoralizing, or destructive ways. However, similar to other types of abusive people, when UBsers™ do act out, it can be devastating.

Strong women have times when they act out as well. They are human too. For strong women this is not a life strategy.

It can be a conundrum for many women who want to be an understanding, compassionate boss but who do not know or have been taught how to go beyond these strategies for interacting with other women.

Chapter Six
THE EFFECTS OF TIRE TRACKS AND UBS™ ON BUSINESS

Corporations, companies, agencies, small businesses
The adverse effects of woman with UBS™ on Fortune 500 companies, to government agencies, to small businesses can be devastating. Innovation, creativity, collaboration and communication can be crippled by UBS™. Morale and productivity begin to suffer. If UBS™ in one or two women continues without consequences for the UBSers™, ultimately their victims quit or stop giving their input. The ultimate effect on businesses is loss of profitability and their reputation. This can be especially devastating for small or medium businesses.

Women with UBS™
There are several long-term, adverse effects for women who have UBS™. First and foremost, it affects their spiritual and emotional growth. They are entirely run by what they "do and have" such as material wealth, power, prestige, titles, and entitlements. They are not motivated by their state of being. However, if it is truly analyzed, the "having and the doing" is to enhance their being. The being translates into what might be viewed as esoteric but essential such a peaceful, serene, present, content, fulfilled, loving, forgiving, and centered.

"Carefully watch your thoughts, for they become your words. Manage and watch your words, for they will become your actions. Consider and judge your actions, for they have become your habits. Acknowledge and watch your habits, for they shall become your values. Understand and embrace your values, for they become your destiny." — Mahatma Gandhi

Another adverse effect is continually seeking but never being satisfied with a millions of forms of external validation. This rears its ugly head with the obsession of "more". More titles, more awards, more accolades, more money, more real estate, more press. Moreover, it's become such a way of behavior; it's no longer considered a compulsion. It's a habit that has become part of their character.

Often women with UBS™, believe they have many women friends and their life is fulfilled. In giving themselves an honest appraisal, most of them find that they compete or are condescending to almost every woman they come across. They have very few women friends, if any. They may have a million acquaintances, a large amount of women in their social networks both online and in person, but only a few or no true friends. This is because they don't know how to be friends or form friendships because they are so self-centered, manipulative and unaware.

We've all heard the phrase that it's lonely at the top. This phrase holds especially true for women with UBS™. When speaking with Chris Liaguno about this book, he told me that very few women who exhibit UBS™ will read this book. He said it will be primarily read by women who have experienced a boss or co-worker who threw them under the bus. I've included this section on the off chance that women with UBS™ will read it.

It is lonely knowing that you are alienating the women around you or throwing them under the bus figuratively just to get some perceived advantage or gain. It must be exhausting competing with other women and depleting them of their power on a day-by-day basis.

In speaking with a woman who has UBS™, she told me that she was really lonely but she truly didn't like other women. She felt threatened by them and therefore, intimidated. Ultimately, she said she had a girl in middle school bully her because she was getting more attention from the boys. "It haunted me in high school as she turned a lot of other girls against me too. I thought I will never get close to another girl again because of the hurt that bully caused me. It makes me especially want to compete and beat any women in business. I only became aware of my behavior after thinking back about it with you," she continued.

Women who are victims of women with UBS™
There are several long-term adverse effects for women who have been victims of other women with UBS™. First and foremost, women who have been victims of other women with this syndrome begin to lose faith in their own abilities, question

their decisions, and wonder what they are doing wrong. The irrational behavior of their female bosses and co-workers needs to be rationalized so they can make sense of it. It's hard to swallow that you are being treated badly solely on the basis that you are a woman, competent, intelligent, attractive, a hard worker, or for receiving positive attention from others within the company.

Several of the women who I interviewed during the course of writing this book mentioned how depressed they were when they were let go by their boss or when they decided to quit. They played scenarios of mistreatment over and over again in their heads. They often were obsessed about how well the company or organization was doing after they left – speaking with former co-workers, checking stock quotes or reading articles about the companies. These women questioned their abilities, skill sets, and wondered if they were the intimidating ones as opposed to their bosses.

The women who were fired or laid off as a result of a boss with UBS™ experienced financial hardship as well. This coupled with a lack of self-esteem made it difficult for these women to continue to be motivated to search for a new job. It would make them distrust potential female employers. Once hired, they were very guarded with their female supervisors.

"It's appears to be a mild form of post-traumatic stress disorder," says Liaguno. There are a percentage of women who believe they are re-experiencing the trauma they were exposed to at the hands of a boss with UBS™. It can cause undue anxiety and stress. These women may not take a job solely based on the fact that their boss would be a woman. If they take a job, they may believe their boss is distrustful just because they have had a prior female boss with UBS™.

The other effect and perhaps the most disconcerting is when a victim of UBS™ becomes a perpetrator. They watched how their boss appeared to succeed in the company by throwing others under the bus and decide this is how women are in business. This especially holds true when the experience with a boss with UBS™ happens to a woman when she is starting out in her career.

From the interviews:
- "She spoke so ill about me that I could not get another government job in the state. My reputation was ruined. " - Tammy

- "What Brooke did to me when she threw me under the bus still affects me to this day. It happened years ago but I lost a big chunk of my confidence and I don't think I'll ever get it back." - Charlene

The residual effects on the victims of UBS™ can very pronounced or may vary subtly appear over time. The residual effects of UBS™ on companies can be subtle or devastating. Regardless, it is causing women to leave jobs or stop being productive and that will always have an effect to any organization's bottom line.

It's like anything else that threatens the livelihood of an ecosystem. Initially the threat is small or subtle, but left unchecked, over time, it can permeate entire departments, branch offices, and corporations. Any time, any of us deal with someone who is completely unaware of how her words and behavior affects others; there is a potentially very toxic environment.

The fact that these women who are UBSers™ have used the Under the Bus Syndrome™ strategies for so long and have achieved some type of perceived gain, they are not going to stop unless there are dire consequences, or they awaken to their behaviors.

The victims of the UBSer™ often cannot leave their jobs, the department, or the project and will begin to suffer in silence. They not only lose confidence in themselves but they hold back their creative or innovative ideas and processes because they are in fear of losing their job, credibility, or promotion. These victims also start to question the management team and wonder why they tolerate that type of behavior.

Women have difficulty in blaming themselves when they are victimized by women with UBS™. "You will hear women say that if only I was more skilled or if I worked harder on the project. I shouldn't have made her mad by being so efficient on that project," said Liaguno. He continues that this behavior is very similar to victims of domestic violence. The victims want to blame themselves or some other outside influence for the abusers' behavior. The majority of women who I interviewed [whether their stories are in this book or not] speak of the long lasting effects that the UBSers™' behavior and words have on them.

Most common residual effects of women who experienced another woman with UBS™:
- Replaying or reliving the scenario(s) over and over again in their minds
- Loss of self-esteem, confidence and self-worth
- Apathy towards job, department, management team and company.
- Low morale and feelings of distrust
- Limited communication or no longer communicating with fellow employees or management
- Loss of appetite or overeating, loss of sleep, nightmares, depression and sadness

- Having reputation tainted at the company, with other business professionals or within a particular industry – otherwise known as black balled

The two effects that are most profound or most impactful to businesses and individuals are: 1. Women who leave their jobs because of the UBSer; 2. Women who never truly gain their confidence back and have a difficult time trusting other women in business ever again. Both of these effects not only hurt all the advances that women have made in business, but they slowly chip away at any future progress.

The women who cause the harm can change, but they must be willing to change. And, as it is said in literally all recovery programs, the first step is for the UBSer to admit, she has a problem. Everyone else around her cannot admit it for her or take responsibility for her toxic behavior.

It is said that we can only grow if we change. This is the reason; I am almost six feet tall. I've had to change continuously throughout my career. I call them A.F.G.'s™ – another freaking growth experience™.

Another Freaking Growth Experience™ or AFG™

This term is used when a woman experiences a time when she has grown mentally, emotionally, intellectually or spiritually. However, that growth has either been painful or at a cost. In some cases, it's termed as such due to the woman repeating mistakes over and over then finally changing and growing from the experience.

Are you ready for an AFG™?
Sign up for one of my workshops at underthebusnomore.com.
In the next chapter, we will get on the bus and look at driving to a better future for women in business.

Chapter Seven:
GET ON THE BUS AND DRIVE TOWARD A BETTER FUTURE

The Pledge – No More UBS™
When I find myself having the need to harm, hinder, or halt the progress of a woman colleague, co-worker, client, or vendor due to my own UBS™, I will be aware of it and stop. I will look inside myself for internal validation and I will seek help to change it.

The Pledge – Woman to Woman Responsibility
I am responsible. When any woman, anywhere in business reaches out for my help, I will take the time to share my knowledge, experience, and connections; to always be there to lift her up and mentor her success. And for that mentorship, I am responsible.

To sign the pledge online, go to underthebusnomore.com

Chapter Eight:
TO A BETTER FUTURE

Fortunately for all of us, there are several women's organizations that are being formed all the time to assist women to empower themselves and seek their highest potential.

It is a great blessing to all women that women like Rosa Parks (Civil rights heroine), Gloria Steinem (women's advocate in the 1960s and 70s), the women who were part of the suffrage movement (women's voting rights) who worked so hard for freedoms paved the road before us.

We need to take a moment to reflect on these women with gratitude and blessings and know that if we become aware of our actions/thoughts, we can change them. We can teach our daughters, sisters, family, friends, and ourselves how to have self-validating life strategies, we can do what we're passionate about and we can mentor others to do the same.

It is my greatest hope that this book helps to bring about healing and empowerment of women. Yes, it's a lofty goal. I will end with one more driving analogy. The rear view mirror is small because it represents the past. And, it's behind you. The windshield is large because you are driving forward toward a big and ever expanding future.

www.ingramcontent.com/pod-product-compliance
Lightning Source LLC
Chambersburg PA
CBHW070819180526
45168CB00002B/686